Simple
FRENCH
COOKING

CHUCK WILLIAMS
COLLECTION

RECIPES BY CHUCK WILLIAMS

PHOTOGRAPHS BY ALLAN ROSENBERG

WELDON OWEN

First published in the USA in 1996 by
Weldon Owen Inc.
814 Montgomery Street
San Francisco, CA 94133

In collaboration with Williams-Sonoma
3250 Van Ness Avenue, San Francisco, CA 94109

The Chuck Williams Collection
conceived and produced by Weldon Owen Inc.

WILLIAMS-SONOMA
Founder/Vice-Chairman: Chuck Williams

WELDON OWEN INC.
President: John Owen
Vice President and Publisher: Wendely Harvey
Vice President and CFO: Richard VanOosterhout
Associate Publisher: Laurie Wertz
Consulting Editor: Norman Kolpas
Copy Editor: Sharon Silva
Design: John Bull, The Book Design Company
Design Layout: Janique Gascoigne
Production Director: Stephanie Sherman
Production Coordinator: Tarji Mickelson
Production Editor: Janique Gascoigne
Co-Editions Director: Derek Barton
Photography: Allan Rosenberg
Additional Photography: Allen V. Lott
Prop Stylist: Sandra Griswold
Food Stylist: Heidi Gintner
Assistant Food Stylists: Nette Scott, William Shaw
Assistant Food & Prop Stylist: Elizabeth C. Davis
Illustrations: Alice Harth

Library of Congress Cataloging-in-Publication Data:

Williams, Chuck.
    Simple French cooking / recipes by Chuck Williams ;
photographs by Allan Rosenberg.
        p.   cm. — (Chuck Williams collection)
    Includes index.
    ISBN 1-875137-10-6
    1. Cookery, French.   I. Title.
    II. Series: Williams, Chuck.
    Chuck Williams collection.
    TX719.W557   1995
    641.5944—dc20   95-46408
                                           CIP

Production by Mandarin Offset, Hong Kong
Printed in China

A Note on Weights & Measures:
All recipes include customary US, UK and
metric measurements. Conversions are
based on a standard developed for these
books and have been rounded off. Actual
weights may vary.

CONTENTS

Introduction

When I first visited France, in 1952, I was bowled over by foods I'd never seen before. I remember *coq au vin,* that classic dish of chicken braised in red wine; *boeuf bourguignon,* the legendary beef stew of Burgundy; steaming pots of lentils and flageolets.

Soufflés, both savory and sweet, were completely new to me. I'll never forget one in particular: It was baked in a grapefruit shell, and was absolutely delicious.

The breads, too, were memorable. In the morning, I would sit in a sidewalk café and have a croissant or a piece of baguette still warm from the oven, accompanied by a *café au lait* or a big cup of hot chocolate.

America's love affair with French cooking was just beginning to take off in the late 1950s, when I first started Williams-Sonoma. The next decade, I watched interest grow wildly thanks to Julia Child, who gave loyal television viewers a weekly infusion of the cuisine. It seemed that many people were talking about what French dishes they were going to cook that night or next weekend—the cheese soufflés and omelets and quiches, and all those wine-scented stews and braises.

Today, of course, much of that food seems quaint to us. Our finest restaurants and more homespun regional American cooking alike have absorbed the lessons of the French kitchen and made them their own.

What have we learned? I think the strong familiarity of the dishes in this book—an entirely personal collection of my favorite, easy French recipes—offers an answer. You'll find here simple salads lightly coated with fragrant vinaigrettes. Appetizers and soups that highlight fresh ingredients. Honest, country-style roasts, stews, sautés and braises of poultry, seafood and meat, many of which gain extra character from good wine. Imaginative and versatile vegetable side dishes. Desserts that, for the most part, are light and feature in-season fruits. And, yes, even a classic soufflé and an easy omelet.

Seasonality. Freshness. Imagination. Honesty. Simplicity. These are the hallmarks of French cooking that first impressed me more than four decades ago—characteristics that have indelibly marked the way we all think about food today.

The very familiarity of the recipes makes this book exceptionally easy to use, and they're easier still for the useful cooking tips I've included with each one. Feel free to incorporate these dishes into your own daily cooking; a single one can make a meal more enjoyable. Or use them to compose an entire French menu, whether for a casual family occasion or a special party; I offer some sample menus on page 119 to help inspire you. You'll also find guides to the French-style equipment that is so readily available today, as well as to cooking techniques and ingredients that will come in handy.

When the topic of French food comes up, wine almost immediately follows. Besides the wealth of good imported French wines, there are, of course, world-class wines from America and other countries. The wisest counsel I can offer is to find a wine that you like and enjoy it with your meal.

That done, please join me in raising a glass and saying, *"Bon appétit!"*

Asparagus with Orange Hollandaise Sauce

Hollandaise, the classic sauce for dressing warm asparagus in France, is usually flavored with lemon. The orange juice used in this recipe is a nice change of pace, and goes particularly well with the vegetable.

The sauce is easy to make—I think even easier than mayonnaise. Just keep in mind these few simple tips: Make it over simmering water instead of over direct heat; too much heat will only cook the egg yolk rather than thicken the sauce. A bowl rather than the top pan of a double boiler contributes to a smoother whisking of the sauce. And finally, I find that softened butter blends in more readily than the more commonly used melted butter.

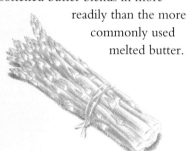

FOR THE ORANGE HOLLANDAISE SAUCE:
2 egg yolks
3 tablespoons fresh orange juice
6 tablespoons (3 oz/90 g) unsalted butter, cut into slices
 ¼ inch (6 mm) thick, at room temperature
Salt and freshly ground pepper

1½ lb (750 g) asparagus spears
2 teaspoons salt
1 orange

To make the sauce, place the egg yolks and 2 tablespoons of the orange juice in a heatproof bowl or the top pan of a double boiler. Set the bowl or pan over (but not touching) hot or barely simmering water in a saucepan or the bottom pan of the double boiler. Whisk continuously until warm and just beginning to thicken, about 1 minute. Add the butter, 1 slice at a time, whisking until fully absorbed before adding the next slice. When all of the butter is absorbed, continue to whisk until thickened, 2–3 minutes. Do not overcook.

❧ Remove the bowl or pan from the pan of hot water; season to taste with salt and pepper. If the sauce is too thick, stir in as much of the remaining 1 tablespoon orange juice as needed to thin to desired consistency. You should have about ¾ cup (6 fl oz/180 ml) sauce. Remove the bottom pan from the heat and let the water cool slightly. Then replace the hollandaise over the warm water and cover loosely with a paper towel (this prevents a skin from forming).

❧ Cut or break off the tough white ends from the asparagus spears. Trim all the spears to the same length. If the spears are large, use a vegetable peeler to peel away the tough skin as well, starting 2 inches below the tip.

❧ Select a large sauté pan or frying pan that will hold the asparagus in a single layer. Fill half full with water and place over high heat. Bring to a boil and add the salt and asparagus. Bring back to a boil, reduce the heat slightly and boil gently, uncovered, until just tender when pierced with a knife tip, 6–9 minutes, depending upon the size of the spears. Remove from the heat and drain well.

❧ To serve, immediately divide the asparagus among 4 warmed plates, arranging the spears in a row, and spoon the warm hollandaise sauce in a wide stripe across the middle of the asparagus. Using a zester or fine-holed shredder, and holding the orange over each serving, shred a little zest from the orange peel directly over the hollandaise on each serving (see glossary, page 126). Serve immediately.

SERVES 4

Green Lentil Salad

1 cup (7 oz/220 g) dried green lentils
3 cups (24 fl oz/750 ml) water
1 small white sweet onion, stuck with 2 whole cloves
1 bay leaf
1 orange zest strip, 1 inch (2.5 cm) wide and 2 inches (5 cm) long

FOR THE DRESSING:
2 tablespoons tarragon white wine vinegar
⅛ teaspoon salt
Freshly ground pepper
1 teaspoon Dijon-style mustard
⅓ cup (3 fl oz/80 ml) extra-virgin olive oil

1 carrot, peeled and shredded
½ green bell pepper (capsicum), seeded, deribbed and cut into
   small dice (½ cup/2½ oz/75 g)
1 tablespoon minced green (spring) onion, including some tender
   green tops (2 or 3 onions)
8 tender romaine (cos) lettuce leaves, carefully washed and dried

Sort through the lentils, discarding any misshapen lentils or small stones. Rinse, drain and place in a saucepan. Add the water, onion, bay leaf and orange zest and place over medium-high heat. Bring to a boil, reduce the heat to medium-low, cover partially and simmer until the lentils are tender, 30–35 minutes. Remove from the heat and remove and discard the onion, bay leaf and orange zest. Drain the lentils well and transfer them to a bowl. Set aside to cool completely.
To make the dressing, in a small bowl, combine the vinegar and salt and stir until the salt dissolves. Add pepper to taste and the mustard and whisk until blended. Gradually add the olive oil, whisking until well blended and emulsified. Taste and adjust the seasoning. Set aside.
Add the carrot, bell pepper and green onion to the cooled lentils. Toss until well mixed. Drizzle with the dressing and toss again. Taste and adjust the seasonings.
To serve, arrange 2 lettuce leaves on each of 4 salad plates. Spoon an equal portion of the lentils onto each plate. Serve at room temperature.

SERVES 4

An excellent first course for a weekend brunch, this salad may also be served as a luncheon main course, preceded by a soup. It can be made several hours ahead and refrigerated. Bring to room temperature and stir before serving.

Small dark green lentils, exported from France and also known as Puy lentils, are essential for this recipe. Green lentils are now being grown in the United States as well. You'll find them in specialty-food stores and in the international-food sections of large markets.

LEEKS À LA GRECQUE

2 lb (1 kg) young, slender leeks
Salt
8–10 small pearl onions
¾ cup (6 fl oz/180 ml) chicken broth or water, or as needed
⅓ cup (3 fl oz/80 ml) dry white wine
3 tablespoons olive oil
1 tablespoon tomato paste
4 bay leaves
1 teaspoon peppercorns
Paprika

Following the directions on page 125, trim the leeks, leaving about 1 inch (2.5 cm) of the tender green tops, then rinse them. If the leeks are small, leave them whole; if they are medium-sized, cut them in half lengthwise.

Gather the leeks together in a bundle and tie in 2 or 3 places with kitchen string to secure the bundle. Fill a large, wide pot half full with water and bring to a boil. Add 1 tablespoon salt and the bundle of leeks and boil, uncovered, for 5 minutes. Drain the leeks and let cool for a few minutes. When cool enough to handle, snip the strings and separate the leeks. Set aside.

Fill a small saucepan three-fourths full with water and bring to a boil. Add the pearl onions and boil, uncovered, for 3 minutes. Drain the onions and immerse them in cold water. Using a small, sharp knife, trim the root ends and cut a shallow X in the root ends. Using your fingers, slip off the skins. Set aside.

In a large sauté pan or frying pan that will hold the leeks in a single layer, arrange the leeks in a row. In a small bowl, combine the ¾ cup (6 fl oz/180 ml) broth, the wine, olive oil and tomato paste. Stir until well blended and then pour the broth mixture over the leeks. Tuck the bay leaves under the leeks and scatter the peppercorns over the top. Arrange the onions around and among the leeks so that they sit in the liquid. The liquid should reach just to the top of the leeks; add more broth if necessary.

Place the pan over medium heat and bring to a simmer. Reduce the heat to low and allow the liquid to barely simmer, uncovered, until the leeks are tender when pierced with a knife and the liquid is reduced to a few spoonfuls, about 45 minutes. Remove from the heat and set aside to cool completely.

To serve, arrange the leeks in a row in a serving dish. Arrange the onions and bay leaves over the leeks and spoon the reduced sauce, including the peppercorns, over the leeks and onions. Sprinkle with paprika and serve at room temperature.

SERVES 4

NOTES

This splendid first course is loved the world over—and no more so than in France. An excellent cold dish, it is easily prepared and adds a touch of casual elegance to any warm-weather meal.

The dish will be at its best when made with small, tender leeks. If tiny pearl onions are out of season, use the smallest boiling onions you can find—no more than 1 inch (2.5 cm) in diameter—and cut them in half vertically, through their stem and root ends, so the halves hold together.

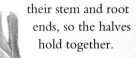

NOTES

The French call this refreshing first-course salad *céleri-rave rémoulade*. You'll find it on many bistro menus. Celery root is a winter vegetable, so this makes an excellent lunch dish or dinner first course when there is a shortage of fresh salad vegetables.

If by chance the mayonnaise mixture separates when you begin to add oil, start over again with another egg yolk. If the mixture separates when half or more of the oil has been beaten in, the mayonnaise can be saved by putting another egg yolk in a clean bowl and vigorously beating in a little of the separated mixture until emulsified and smooth, then beating in the rest of the mixture a little at a time. Then beat in the rest of the oil plus additional oil until very thick.

CELERY ROOT WITH MUSTARD MAYONNAISE

FOR THE MUSTARD MAYONNAISE:
1 egg yolk, at room temperature
1 tablespoon Dijon-style mustard
⅛ teaspoon salt
Dash of cayenne pepper
½ cup (4 fl oz/125 ml) light olive oil or vegetable oil
2 tablespoons fresh lemon juice
1–2 tablespoons heavy (double) cream

1 celery root, about 1 lb (500 g)

To make the mustard mayonnaise, in a bowl, combine the egg yolk, mustard, salt and cayenne pepper. Using a whisk, beat until well blended. Add a little oil and whisk vigorously until an emulsion forms. Add a little more oil and again whisk vigorously to ensure the emulsion is stabilized. Then continue to add oil, a little at a time, beating vigorously after each addition until it is absorbed. When all of the oil has been beaten in, the sauce should be very thick. Add the lemon juice and whisk to mix well. Whisk in 1 tablespoon cream. Add more cream as needed to attain a creamy sauce. Taste and adjust the seasonings. Set aside.

Using a sharp paring knife, peel the celery root, removing all of the brown skin. Then, using the medium holes on a hand-held shredder, shred the celery root. Immediately put the shredded celery root into a bowl and add about one-half of the mustard mayonnaise. Mix well. Add more of the mayonnaise as necessary to coat the celery root lightly.

Spoon onto individual plates and serve immediately.

SERVES 4

VEGETABLES WITH THREE SAUCES

1 fennel bulb, trimmed, old or bruised leaves removed
½ lb (250 g) young green beans, trimmed and cut in half if long
Ice water to cover
1 small head cauliflower, cut into florets, large florets halved
1 slender English (hothouse) cucumber
1 tablespoon tarragon white wine vinegar
Salt and freshly ground pepper
⅔ cup (5 fl oz/160 ml) extra-virgin olive oil
1 tablespoon red wine vinegar
1 teaspoon Dijon-style mustard
½ cup (4 fl oz/125 ml) sour cream
2 teaspoons chopped fresh dill
½–1 tablespoon fresh lemon juice
3 young carrots, about ½ lb (250 g) total weight, peeled and shredded
½ lb (250 g) cherry tomatoes, stems removed
3 sprigs each of any 3 of the following fresh herbs: tarragon, mint,
   dill, flat-leaf (Italian) parsley, basil and lemon thyme

Cut the fennel bulb in half lengthwise through the narrow side. Cut each half crosswise into slices ⅛ inch (3 mm) thick. Set aside. Place the green beans in a bowl, add ice water to cover and set aside to crisp for 10–15 minutes.

Fill a saucepan three-fourths full with water and bring to a boil. Using tongs, transfer the green beans to the boiling water; reserve the ice water. Boil, uncovered, until bright green but still crisp, 3–4 minutes. Using the tongs, return the beans to the ice water. Add the cauliflower florets to the boiling water and boil until about half tender, 3–4 minutes. Drain; set aside to cool. Drain the green beans; set aside.

Peel the cucumber and cut lengthwise into quarters, then cut each quarter in half lengthwise. If the seeds are large, use a small knife to remove the seed core. Cut the strips into 2–2½-inch (5–6-cm) lengths. Set aside.

Make the 3 sauces: In a small bowl, whisk together the tarragon vinegar, ⅛ teaspoon salt, and pepper to taste. Gradually add ⅓ cup (2½ fl oz/80 ml) of the olive oil, whisking well. Set aside. In another small bowl, whisk together the red wine vinegar, mustard, and salt and pepper to taste. Gradually add the remaining ⅓ cup (2½ fl oz/80 ml) olive oil, whisking well. Set aside. In a third small bowl, whisk together the sour cream, chopped dill, lemon juice and salt and pepper to taste.

To serve, arrange the shredded carrots, fennel and the bowl of tarragon vinaigrette on a serving dish. On a second dish, arrange the green beans, cauliflower and the mustard vinaigrette. On a third dish, arrange the tomatoes, cucumber strips and the dill cream sauce. Garnish each dish with the herb sprigs.

SERVES 4

NOTES

Crudités, the most popular of all first courses in France, are assortments of raw vegetables that have been cut, sliced or shredded to make them easy to eat. I have taken the liberty here of blanching two of the vegetables—cauliflower and green beans—for better flavor, color and texture.

In this recipe, I present three combinations of two vegetables each, and each pair has its own simple dressing. Served together, they make an excellent first course for a buffet lunch or an early evening party.

The tarragon white wine vinegar adds a marvelously fragrant flavor. Look for it in specialty-food shops and some well-stocked food stores.

LEEK AND POTATO SOUP

One of the most comforting of all hot soups, leek and potato is also one of the most delicious when served cold—as the classic recipe called vichyssoise—on a warm day. I have added carrot to the traditional recipe to enhance the color and flavor.

I call for a food mill to purée the soup. This simple kitchen tool gives it a more substantial texture than if it were puréed in a food processor or blender, but you can certainly use those machines if you like.

1 lb (500 g) leeks (about 3 medium)
2 tablespoons unsalted butter
1 lb (500 g) baking potatoes, peeled and cubed
2 carrots, peeled and sliced
Salt and freshly ground pepper
¼ cup (2 fl oz/60 ml) heavy (double) cream if serving hot
   or ½ cup (4 fl oz/125 ml) cream if serving cold
4 thin lemon slices
Fresh chives

Following the directions on page 125, trim the leeks, leaving about 1 inch (2.5 cm) of the tender green tops, then rinse them. Cut crosswise into slices ½ inch (12 mm) thick.

In a large saucepan over medium-low heat, melt the butter. When foaming, add the leeks and sauté, stirring occasionally, until they have wilted a little, 3–4 minutes. Add the potatoes and carrots, then add water just to cover the vegetables. Raise the heat to medium and bring to a boil. Reduce the heat to low and simmer, uncovered, until the vegetables are tender when pierced with the tip of a knife, about 30 minutes.

Fit a food mill with the medium disk and rest the mill over a large bowl. Using a ladle or a large spoon and working in batches, transfer the cooked vegetables and their liquid to the food mill and turn the handle to purée.

If serving the soup hot, return the puréed vegetables to the saucepan and season to taste with salt and pepper. Return the saucepan to medium-low heat, stir in ¼ cup (2 fl oz/60 ml) cream and heat to just under a boil. Add a little water if the purée is too thick. Taste and adjust the seasonings.

Ladle into warmed bowls and float a lemon slice on top of each serving. Using scissors, cut the chives into pieces ¼ inch (6 mm) long and sprinkle the chives on the lemon slice. Serve at once.

To serve cold, do not return the purée to the saucepan. Instead, cover the bowl and refrigerate until well chilled. When ready to serve, season to taste with salt and pepper and stir in ½ cup (4 fl oz/125 ml) cream, mixing well. Taste and adjust the seasonings. Ladle into chilled individual bowls. Float a lemon slice on top of each serving and garnish with the chives as directed above.

SERVES 4

CARROT SOUP WITH CORIANDER

10–12 carrots, 1–1½ lb (500–750 g) total weight
1 baking potato, 8–9 oz (250–280 g)
2 oz (60 g) shallots (3 or 4 shallots)
6 tablespoons (3 oz/90 g) unsalted butter
¾ teaspoon ground coriander
3 cups (24 fl oz/750 ml) chicken broth
½ teaspoon sugar
¼ teaspoon salt
1 cup (8 fl oz/250 ml) milk, or as needed
Freshly ground pepper
2–3 tablespoons dry sherry
About ½ cup (4 fl oz/125 ml) crème fraîche or sour cream
4 tablespoons chopped fresh cilantro (fresh coriander)

Peel the carrots and cut crosswise into pieces ½ inch (12 mm) thick. Peel the potato and cut into small cubes. Cut the shallots crosswise into thin slices. Set aside.

In a large saucepan over medium-low heat, melt the butter. Add the shallots and sauté, stirring occasionally, until softened, 2–3 minutes; do not allow to brown. Add the carrots, potato and coriander and sauté, stirring a couple of times, for 2–3 minutes. Add the chicken broth, sugar and salt. Raise the heat to medium and bring to a simmer. Reduce the heat to low, cover partially and gently simmer until the vegetables are soft when pierced with the tip of a knife, 20–25 minutes.

Remove from the heat and let cool slightly. Working in batches, ladle into a food processor fitted with the metal blade or into a blender. Process to form a smooth purée. Return the purée to the saucepan and add the 1 cup (8 fl oz/ 250 ml) milk and pepper to taste. Place over medium heat and heat until just beginning to simmer. Taste and adjust the seasonings. If too thick, add more milk. Just before serving, stir in the sherry to taste.

Ladle into warmed soup bowls. Top each bowl with 1–2 spoonfuls crème fraîche or sour cream and a generous sprinkling of cilantro.

SERVES 4

Coriander, an intriguing Middle Eastern spice popular in France, adds excellent flavor to carrots. Fresh leaves of cilantro (coriander in its fresh form) make the soup even livelier. Sherry, stirred in just before serving, and a garnish of crème fraîche, a thick, slightly soured French-style cultured cream found in specialty-food shops, contribute further dimensions of flavor.

The potato acts as a necessary thickening agent. Alternatively, you could use 1 cup (5 oz/155 g) cooked white rice.

For a special garnish, make thin carrot curls with a vegetable peeler.

VEGETABLE SOUP WITH TOMATO-BASIL SAUCE

NOTES

Tomato-basil sauce gives this vegetable soup its special aroma and flavor. The sauce is known in France as *pistou,* although it is more commonly made without the addition of tomatoes. You may notice a similarity to Italy's pesto sauce, a good example of how many preparations found in the south of France are common to other Mediterranean countries, with only slight variations in ingredients.

Fresh basil is absolutely necessary for the sauce; the dried herb just does not have the same flavor. If you cannot find fresh oregano or marjoram for the soup, however, you can substitute ½ teaspoon of the dried herb.

1 lb (500 g) ripe tomatoes
½ bunch large-leaved spinach, about ½ lb (250 g)
2 tablespoons olive oil
1 yellow onion, cut into ¼-inch (6-mm) dice (about 1 cup/4 oz/125 g)
1 lb (500 g) baking potatoes, peeled and cut into ½-inch (12-mm) dice
   (about 2 cups/10 oz/315 g)
3 or 4 carrots, peeled and cut into ½-inch (12-mm) dice
   (1–1½ cups/5–7½ oz/155–235 g)
2 tablespoons coarsely chopped fresh parsley, preferably flat-leaf (Italian)
Leaves from 3 fresh oregano or marjoram sprigs, chopped
6 cups (48 fl oz/1.5 l) chicken broth, or as needed
Salt and freshly ground pepper
Tomato-Basil Sauce *(recipe on page 118)*
3 small zucchini (courgettes), trimmed and cut into ½-inch (12-mm) dice
½ lb (250 g) small green beans, trimmed and cut into 2-inch (5-cm) lengths

Core, peel and seed the tomatoes (see glossary, page 124). Chop coarsely; you should have about 2 cups (12 oz/375 g). Set aside.

Rinse the spinach thoroughly. Pick over and discard any old or damaged leaves and remove the stems and discard. Gather the leaves into a stack and, using a sharp knife, cut crosswise into strips ½ inch (12 mm) wide. You should have about 2 cups (3 oz/90 g), packed. Set aside.

In a large saucepan or stew pot over medium-low heat, warm the olive oil. When hot, add the onion and sauté, stirring occasionally, until translucent, 6–8 minutes. Add the tomatoes, potatoes, carrots, parsley, and oregano or marjoram and cover. Let steam for 4–5 minutes. Add 6 cups (48 fl oz/1.5 l) chicken broth and salt and pepper to taste. Raise the heat to medium and bring to a simmer. Reduce the heat to low, cover partially and simmer gently until the potatoes and carrots are almost tender, 15–20 minutes.

Meanwhile, prepare the Tomato-Basil Sauce.

When the vegetables are almost tender, add the zucchini and green beans, plus more chicken broth if needed to cover the vegetables. Continue to simmer until the beans are just tender, 8–10 minutes. Add the spinach and simmer for another few minutes until it wilts. Taste and adjust the seasonings.

Ladle into warmed soup bowls and top each serving with a spoonful of Tomato-Basil Sauce. Serve any remaining sauce in a bowl at the table.

SERVES 4

CREAM OF MUSHROOM SOUP

1 lb (500 g) small, firm fresh mushrooms, preferably brown
¼ cup (2 oz/60 g) unsalted butter
2 tablespoons chopped shallots (about 2 small shallots)
1 small white sweet onion, chopped (about ½ cup/2½ oz/75 g)
1 white potato, peeled and cut into ½-inch (12-mm) dice
   (about 1 cup/5 oz/155 g)
2 cups (16 fl oz/500 ml) chicken broth
Salt
1 cup (8 fl oz/250 ml) heavy (double) cream
2–3 tablespoons Madeira wine, preferably imported
Freshly grated nutmeg
Freshly ground pepper
2 oz (60 g) Brie cheese, rind removed and sliced into 10–12 thin pieces
Chopped fresh basil

Using a soft brush or clean kitchen towel, brush off any soil or other impurities from the mushrooms. Do not rinse in water. Trim the stems and chop the mushrooms coarsely; set aside.

In a sauté pan or large saucepan over medium-low heat, melt the butter. Add the shallots and onion and simmer, stirring occasionally, until soft and translucent, 5–6 minutes. Add the mushrooms, increase the heat to medium and sauté, stirring and tossing, until the mushrooms begin to release their liquid, 8–10 minutes; do not allow the onions to brown. Add the potato, chicken broth and salt to taste, cover partially and simmer until the mushrooms and potato are soft, 15–20 minutes, adjusting the heat if necessary to maintain a simmer.

Remove from the heat and let cool slightly. Working in batches, ladle the soup into a food processor fitted with the metal blade or into a blender. Process the soup to form a smooth purée. Return the purée to the saucepan and add the cream. Place over medium-low heat and bring almost to a simmer; do not allow to boil. Add the Madeira to taste, a little nutmeg and a little pepper. Taste and adjust the seasonings.

Ladle into warmed soup plates or bowls. Float 2 or 3 pieces of the cheese on the surface of each bowl of soup. Sprinkle with chopped basil and serve.

SERVES 4

I've adapted this lovely first-course soup from one that was made for me years ago by my friend Cheryl Schultz, in Dallas, Texas. What impressed me about the recipe then, and still does, is how well it highlights the flavor of the mushrooms—just as a classic French bistro soup should. The potato imparts to the soup all the thickening it needs, and the splash of Madeira provides a special bouquet.

Melting a little Brie cheese on top at serving time adds elegance and richness. Make sure you select a cheese that is ripe and soft, and have it at room temperature so that it will begin to melt the moment you add it.

Select mushrooms with tightly closed caps; there should be no gills showing.

With roots firmly planted in the peasant cooking of such European countries as France, Germany and Holland, split pea soup came to America with the early settlers. It remains a favorite on both sides of the Atlantic, and I have enjoyed it many times in small bistros in Paris and in towns north of the city. I recommend serving it as a simple, satisfying evening meal.

You'll note that sausage is included in the recipe, just as I have found it so often in France. You can, of course, make a vegetarian version by leaving it out. In either case, serve the soup with crusty French bread.

SPLIT PEA SOUP

3 ripe tomatoes, 10–12 oz (315–375 g) total weight
1 large leek
1½ cups (10½ oz/330 g) dried split peas
1 tablespoon olive oil or vegetable oil
1 carrot, peeled and diced (½ cup/2½ oz/75 g)
1 celery stalk, diced (½ cup/2½ oz/75 g)
½ lb (250 g) smoked sausages such as andouille or other flavorful smoked
    sausages made of pork, veal, chicken or turkey
6 cups (48 fl oz/1.5 l) chicken broth or water
½ teaspoon salt
3 fresh parsley sprigs
3 fresh thyme sprigs
1 bay leaf
2 orange zest strips *(see glossary, page 126),* each 2 inches (5 cm) long
    by 1 inch (2.5 cm) wide and each stuck with 1 whole clove
Freshly ground pepper

Core, peel and seed the tomatoes (see glossary, page 124). Chop coarsely; you should have about 1½ cups (9 oz/280 g). Set aside. Trim the leek, leaving about 1 inch (2.5 cm) of the tender green tops, then rinse it (see glossary, page 125). Cut crosswise into ¼-inch (6-mm) slices. Set aside. Sort through the split peas, discarding any damaged peas or small stones. Rinse, drain and set aside.

In a large saucepan over medium-low heat, warm the oil. When hot, add the leek slices and sauté until they begin to wilt, 3–4 minutes. Add the carrot and celery and sauté for 2–3 minutes longer. Add the split peas, tomatoes, whole sausages, broth or water, and salt and stir well. Gather the parsley and thyme sprigs, bay leaf and orange zest strips into a bunch, fold over the stems and tie securely with kitchen string to form a bouquet garni. Add to the pan. Raise the heat and bring to a boil. Reduce the heat to low, cover partially and simmer until the split peas and vegetables are tender, 40–50 minutes.

Let cool slightly. Using tongs, transfer the sausages to a plate. Remove and discard the bouquet. Working in batches, ladle the soup into a food processor fitted with the metal blade or into a blender. Pulse to form a coarse purée and return to the pan. Cut the sausages crosswise into ¼-inch (6-mm) slices and return to the pan. Place over medium heat; bring to a simmer, stirring constantly. Reduce the heat to low and simmer gently for a few minutes. Add pepper to taste and adjust the seasonings.

Ladle into warmed soup bowls and serve at once.

SERVES 4

ONION SOUP

1½–2 lb (750 g–1 kg) yellow onions
¼ cup (2 oz/60 g) unsalted butter
1 tablespoon all-purpose (plain) flour
5 cups (40 fl oz/1.25 l) chicken broth, heated
1 tablespoon molasses
2 fresh parsley sprigs
2 fresh thyme sprigs
1 bay leaf
Salt and freshly ground pepper
Pinch of cayenne pepper
2–3 tablespoons dry sherry
8–12 slices French baguette
1 cup (4 oz/125 g) shredded Gruyère cheese

Peel and cut the onions in half lengthwise. Lay each half on a cutting surface, cut side down, and cut crosswise into slices ¼ inch (6 mm) thick.

In a large, wide saucepan over medium heat, melt the butter. Add the onions and sauté, stirring occasionally, until they are evenly golden, 20–30 minutes.

Sprinkle the flour over the onions; stir and cook until evenly distributed, 1–2 minutes. Raise the heat to medium-high and gradually add the chicken broth, stirring constantly. Continue to stir until the mixture comes to a boil and is smooth and thickened, 3–4 minutes. Add the molasses and stir until blended.

Gather the parsley and thyme sprigs and bay leaf together into a bunch, fold over the stems and tie securely with kitchen string to form a bouquet garni. Add to the pan. Reduce the heat to low, cover partially and simmer gently until the onions are very tender, 30–40 minutes. Season to taste with salt and pepper and with the cayenne.

At serving time, preheat a broiler (griller). Warm 4 deep flameproof soup bowls.

Remove the bouquet from the soup and discard. Stir in sherry to taste. Place the soup bowls on a heavy-duty baking sheet or a broiler pan and ladle the soup into the bowls. Float 2 or 3 baguette slices on top of each bowl. Generously sprinkle the cheese on the bread slices. Place under the broiler, with the cheese topping about 4 inches (10 cm) from the heat source, and broil (grill) until the cheese melts and starts to turn golden, 4–5 minutes. Serve at once.

SERVES 4

NOTES

Nothing tastes better on a cold winter day than a bowl of hot onion soup with its cap of melted cheese concealing a floating baguette slice. All you need for a complete meal is a green salad, a glass of red wine and more bread to sop up the broth.

Make sure that the bowls you use for serving the soup are flameproof. In France, onion soup is served in individual glazed earthenware crocks.

SCALLOP CREAM SOUP

2 tablespoons unsalted butter
2 tablespoons minced shallots (about 2 small shallots)
1 small yellow onion, minced (about ½ cup/2½ oz/75 g)
2 tablespoons all-purpose (plain) flour
3 cups (24 fl oz/750 ml) milk, heated
1 bay leaf
2 fresh thyme sprigs
3 or 4 small, young carrots, peeled and thinly sliced (about 1 cup/4 oz/125 g)
1 lb (500 g) sea scallops or bay scallops, trimmed
1 cup (8 fl oz/250 ml) bottled clam juice
½ cup (4 fl oz/125 ml) dry white wine
1 cup (8 fl oz/250 ml) heavy (double) cream
3 egg yolks
Salt and freshly ground pepper
1 lemon, cut crosswise into thin slices
Chopped fresh parsley or thyme for garnish

In a large saucepan over medium-low heat, melt the butter. Add the shallots and sauté for 1 minute. Add the onion and sauté until translucent, 4–5 minutes. Add the flour and stir until well blended. Cook, stirring, for a few seconds without browning. Gradually add the milk, stirring. Raise the heat to medium and stir until the mixture comes to a boil and is thickened and smooth, 3–4 minutes. Add the bay leaf, thyme and carrots, cover partially and cook gently until the carrots are tender, 15–20 minutes; do not allow to boil. Discard the bay leaf and thyme.
🐚 Meanwhile, if using sea scallops, cut into small pieces or thin slices; leave bay scallops whole. In a small saucepan, combine the clam juice and wine and bring to a boil. Reduce the heat to low and add the scallops. Cover and poach very gently until just opaque, about 2 minutes. Using a slotted spoon, transfer the scallops to a plate and set aside. Reserve the poaching liquid.
🐚 When the carrots are tender, add the poaching liquid to the milk mixture and remove from the heat. In a bowl, combine the cream and egg yolks and beat until blended. Slowly add about 1 cup (8 fl oz/250 ml) of the hot milk mixture to the yolk-cream mixture, stirring constantly until well blended, then add to the soup. Cook over medium-low heat, stirring constantly, until the soup coats the spoon and thickens, 5–6 minutes; do not allow it to boil. Add the scallops and season to taste with salt and pepper. Ladle into warmed bowls. Float lemon slices on each bowl and sprinkle with parsley or thyme. Serve at once.

SERVES 4 AS A MAIN COURSE, 6 AS A FIRST COURSE

NOTES

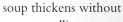

I enjoyed this soup several times in Paris many, many years ago and devised my own recipe for it when I returned home. It goes very well before a simple main course such as grilled lamb chops with asparagus, or quickly seared veal slices with spinach. Or serve it as a main course for a weekend lunch or supper, accompanied by a green salad of young, tender lettuces.

The soup goes together quickly and simply. Just remember that you should have the other courses prepared beforehand, so you can give it your full attention, thus ensuring that the scallops are perfectly poached and that the soup thickens without curdling.

CHICORY AND GOAT CHEESE SALAD

NOTES

Goat's milk cheese, long a favorite on European tables, has only recently become popular in America. Many European countries produce distinctive goat cheeses, from Greece's feta to Italy's *caprini*. French-style *chèvres* may now be found in many cheese shops, in both imported and domestic versions. Be sure to select a soft, fresh variety for this recipe.

Walnut white wine vinegar is, as its name implies, a white wine vinegar infused with the essence of walnuts, producing an excellent flavor that goes well in salad dressings. Several brands are imported from France and may be found in specialty-food shops and in the international sections of large food stores. Tarragon white wine vinegar can be substituted.

½ cup (2 oz/60 g) walnut pieces, broken into small pieces or coarsely chopped
1 tablespoon walnut white wine vinegar
⅛ teaspoon salt
Freshly ground pepper
6 tablespoons (3 fl oz/90 ml) extra-virgin olive oil
1 or 2 heads chicory (curly endive), depending upon size
1 slice coarse country bread or whole-wheat (wholemeal) bread
¼ lb (125 g) fresh goat cheese, preferably *chèvre,* cut into 4 equal slices

Position a rack in the middle of an oven and preheat to 325°F (165°C). Spread the walnut pieces on a baking sheet. Place in the oven and bake until they begin to change color, 6–8 minutes. Watch carefully so they do not burn. Remove from the oven and set aside to cool.

In a small bowl, combine the walnut vinegar, salt, and pepper to taste and stir until the salt dissolves. Gradually add 4 tablespoons (2 fl oz/60 ml) of the olive oil, whisking until well blended. Taste and adjust the seasonings. Set aside.

Separate the leaves from the heads of chicory, discarding any old or damaged leaves. Rinse and dry thoroughly. Tear the leaves into bite-sized pieces and put into a large bowl. Set aside.

Preheat a broiler (griller). Remove the crust from the bread slice and discard. Tear the bread into small pieces and place in a food processor fitted with the metal blade or in a blender. Process to form fine, soft crumbs. Transfer to a saucer. In a separate saucer, place the remaining 2 tablespoons olive oil. Carefully holding 1 slice of cheese at a time, place in the olive oil, turning to coat on all sides. Then place in the bread crumbs and turn to coat thoroughly with the crumbs. Place on a baking sheet and set aside.

Whisk the reserved dressing again until blended and spoon over the lettuce. Toss and turn the leaves until well coated. Divide among 4 plates.

Slip the cheese slices into the broiler about 4 inches (10 cm) from the heat source and broil (grill) until the tops are golden and the cheese has softened, 1–2 minutes. Using a spatula, carefully transfer each slice to the center of a lettuce-lined plate. Sprinkle with the walnut pieces and serve at once.

SERVES 4

MEDITERRANEAN TUNA SALAD

½ lb (250 g) young green beans, trimmed and cut in half crosswise
Ice water to cover
Salt
1 lb (500 g) small, ripe tomatoes
1 cucumber, 9–10 oz (280–315 g)
1 small green bell pepper (capsicum), seeded, deribbed and cut into ½-inch
  (12-mm) squares
4 small green (spring) onions, including some tender green tops, chopped
3–4 tablespoons coarsely chopped fresh dill
2 cans (6½ oz/200 g each) solid-pack tuna in olive oil, drained and flaked
  into small chunks

FOR THE DRESSING:
1 tablespoon fresh lemon juice
1 tablespoon white wine vinegar
Salt and freshly ground pepper
½ cup (4 fl oz/125 ml) extra-virgin olive oil

¼ lb (125 g) mesclun or other small lettuces, carefully rinsed and dried
4 eggs, hard cooked, peeled and quartered lengthwise
8 anchovy fillets in olive oil, drained, rinsed and cut in half crosswise
20–24 tiny Niçoise olives or 12–16 small Italian or Spanish black olives

Place the green beans in a bowl, add ice water to cover and set aside for 10–15
minutes. Fill a saucepan three-fourths full with water and bring to a boil. Add
2 teaspoons salt. Transfer the beans to the pan (reserve the ice water). Boil until
bright green but still crisp, 3–4 minutes. Return the beans to the ice water.
When cool, drain and set aside.

⌘ Core the tomatoes, cut into wedges and put into a bowl. Peel the cucumber,
cut in half lengthwise and, using a melon baller or small spoon, scoop out the
seeds and discard. Cut crosswise into slices ¼ inch (6 mm) thick and add to the
tomatoes. Add the bell pepper, green onions, dill, tuna and green beans.

⌘ To make the dressing, in a small bowl, combine the lemon juice, vinegar,
⅛ teaspoon salt, and pepper to taste. Stir until the salt dissolves. Gradually add the
olive oil, whisking until blended. Spoon half of the dressing over the vegetables
and toss. Taste and adjust the seasonings. Pour the remaining dressing into a bowl.

⌘ Divide the lettuces among 4 plates. Spoon the vegetables on top. Place 4 egg
quarters on each plate and top each quarter with ½ anchovy fillet. Divide the
olives among the salads, then serve. Pass the remaining dressing.

SERVES 4

NOTES

This is my own version of *salade niçoise,* a French salad that enjoys universal appeal. I have added fresh dill, an excellent complement to the tuna. For surrounding the salad, I chose mesclun, the classic Provençal mixture of baby lettuces and herbs, available in well-stocked produce shops or food stores; you can substitute any small lettuces you like.

I know that grilled fresh tuna often appears in Niçoise salads on restaurant menus today. But I still prefer to use canned tuna, which has the best and most traditional flavor for this dish. Look for tuna packed in olive oil.

A French favorite, warm potato salad makes an exceptional accompaniment to hot cooked sausages or to cold meats served at room temperature. It is also very good served on its own.

I find that Yukon Gold potatoes have the best flavor for this salad, and their texture holds together when tossed with the dressing. They are readily available in many markets now. If you cannot find them, use other white potatoes such as White Rose or red new potatoes. The potatoes may be left unpeeled, if you like.

WARM POTATO SALAD

1½ lb (750 g) small boiling potatoes, preferably Yukon Gold
2 teaspoons salt
3 oz (90 g) thickly sliced smoked lean bacon (about 3 slices)

FOR THE DRESSING:
2 tablespoons tarragon white wine vinegar
⅛ teaspoon salt
Freshly ground pepper
⅓ cup (3 fl oz/80 ml) extra-virgin olive oil

2 tablespoons chopped green (spring) onion, including some tender green tops (3 or 4 onions)
2 tablespoons chopped fresh parsley, preferably flat-leaf (Italian)
1 teaspoon chopped fresh tarragon

Scrub the potatoes, but do not peel. Place them in a saucepan and add water to cover and the salt. Bring to a boil over medium-high heat, cover partially and cook until just tender when pierced with the tip of a sharp knife, 20–30 minutes. Drain and let cool slightly.

Meanwhile, cut the bacon crosswise into pieces ¼ inch (6 mm) wide. Place in a heavy frying pan over medium-low heat and fry, stirring occasionally, until golden and crisp, 3–4 minutes. Do not allow to brown too much. Using a slotted spoon, transfer to paper towels to drain. Pour off the fat from the pan, wipe clean with a paper towel and set aside.

To make the dressing, in a small saucepan, combine the vinegar, salt, and pepper to taste and stir until the salt dissolves. Gradually add the olive oil, whisking until well blended. Place over low heat and heat until warm. Set aside and cover to keep warm.

When the potatoes are cool enough to handle, peel them and cut into slices about ½ inch (12 mm) thick. Place in a warmed serving bowl and add the green onion, parsley and tarragon. Toss lightly.

Return the bacon to the reserved pan and place over medium heat to warm. Whisk the warm dressing again and add about three-fourths of it to the potatoes. Toss lightly, adding more dressing if needed. Taste and adjust the seasonings. Garnish with the bacon and serve.

SERVES 4

ENDIVE AND MUSHROOM SALAD WITH MUSTARD DRESSING

2 Belgian endives (chicory), 8–9 oz (250–280 g) total weight
4 green (spring) onions, including some tender green tops
½ lb (250 g) small, firm fresh mushrooms, preferably brown
1 bunch radishes, trimmed and cut into slices ¼ inch (6 mm) thick
1 bunch watercress, carefully rinsed and tough stems removed
½ cup (¾ oz/20 g) coarsely chopped mixed fresh herbs, such as basil,
    tarragon, dill, mint and flat-leaf (Italian) parsley, in any combination

FOR THE DRESSING:
2 tablespoons red wine vinegar
⅛ teaspoon salt
Freshly ground pepper
2 teaspoons Dijon-style mustard
½ cup (4 fl oz/125 ml) extra-virgin olive oil

Trim off any damaged leaves from the endives and discard. Cut the endives crosswise into slices ½ inch (12 mm) thick, discarding the solid heart. Place in a large bowl. Trim and slice the green onions crosswise into 1-inch (2.5-cm) pieces, then slice each piece lengthwise into thin slivers. Add to the bowl.
Using a soft brush or clean kitchen towel, brush off any soil or other impurities from the mushrooms. Do not rinse in water. Trim the stems and cut the mushrooms vertically into slices ¼ inch (6 mm) thick. Add to the bowl along with the radishes, watercress and herbs. Toss to mix.
To make the dressing, in a small bowl, combine the vinegar, salt, and pepper to taste and stir until the salt dissolves. Stir in the mustard until blended. Gradually add the olive oil, whisking until well blended and thickened. Taste and adjust the seasonings.
Drizzle about three-fourths of the dressing over the salad. Toss until well mixed; taste and add more dressing if needed. Store any leftover dressing in a tightly covered container in the refrigerator for up to 3 days. Divide the salad among 4 plates and serve at once.

SERVES 4

NOTES

A salad of many different flavors, this colorful mixture is an excellent prelude to simple grilled meats. The dressing is a traditional French blend of red wine vinegar, olive oil and Dijon mustard, a combination that complements herbs and greens.

Find as many of the fresh herbs as you can. When they are combined in a light salad such as this, the resulting bouquet of tastes and aromas is surprising. Select mushrooms with tightly closed caps; there should be no gills showing.

I was served a salad somewhat like this about thirty years ago in a restaurant in Vallauris, near Nice. Ever since then, I have been creating variations on that memorable dish.

If you do not like to eat beets, the French way of cooking them might change your mind. In France they are baked instead of boiled, which produces a much better flavor. In fact, vegetable markets there sell beets already baked. Do give this simple cooking method a try.

Beet and Orange Salad

4 or 5 medium-sized beets, 2–2½ lb (1–1.25 kg) total weight
2 oranges, preferably seedless navel
1 fennel bulb, 12–14 oz (375–460 g)
1–2 bunches arugula, 7–8 oz (220–250 g), stems removed

For the dressing:
2 tablespoons red wine vinegar
⅛ teaspoon salt
Freshly ground pepper
1½ teaspoons Dijon-style mustard
⅓ cup (3 fl oz/80 ml) extra-virgin olive oil

4 tablespoons shredded fresh basil leaves

Position a rack in the middle of an oven and preheat to 450°F (230°C).

☙ Cut off the tops of the beets, leaving about ½ inch (12 mm) of stem intact. Do not cut off the root ends or otherwise cut into the beets. Rinse well and pat dry. Enclose the beets in a large piece of foil and fold over the top to seal. Make a small slit in the top of the packet and place in a baking pan, folded side up.

☙ Bake until tender when pierced with the tip of a sharp knife, 50–60 minutes depending upon the size and age of the beets; test for doneness after about 45 minutes. Remove from the oven and open the packet partway to let the beets cool a little. When cool enough to handle, cut off the stem and root end from each beet. Using your fingers, or with the aid of a paring knife, peel off the skins; they should slip off easily. Set aside to finish cooling.

☙ Peel and section the oranges (see glossary, page 124). Trim the root end and the stalks from the fennel bulb and remove any old or bruised outer leaves. Cut the bulb crosswise into thin slices. Add to the orange segments. Set aside.

☙ Discard any old or bruised arugula leaves. Rinse carefully and dry well. If large, tear the leaves in half. Place in a separate bowl.

☙ To make the dressing, in a small bowl, combine the vinegar, salt, and pepper to taste. Stir until the salt dissolves. Stir in the mustard until blended and thickened. Gradually add the olive oil, whisking until thickened. Adjust the seasonings. Drizzle about half of the dressing over the arugula and toss well. Set aside.

☙ Thinly slice the beets crosswise. If large, cut in half. Add to the orange segments along with the basil. Drizzle with the remaining dressing and toss gently.

☙ Arrange the arugula leaves on 4 salad plates, dividing them evenly. Spoon the beet-orange-fennel mixture over the top and serve at once.

Serves 4

ESCAROLE SALAD WITH BACON

Very light and simple, this salad makes a nice introduction to a hearty bistro-style main course such as Roast Tarragon Chicken (recipe on page 44).

If you cannot find escarole, chicory (curly endive) may be substituted. Be sure to seek out good smoked lean bacon, preferably freshly cut from a slab by the butcher. If you like, thinly sliced mushrooms or radishes may be added to the salad.

For the best-flavored dressing, use an aged sherry vinegar, or a raspberry white wine vinegar with a good, fresh raspberry flavor and color. Be sure to try the dressing before you add it to the lettuce, and adjust the oil and vinegar proportions to your taste. If your sherry vinegar is not that strong, or if you use raspberry vinegar, you may need to add more vinegar.

1 large or 2 small heads escarole (Batavian endive)
6 oz (185 g) thickly sliced smoked lean bacon (about 6 slices)

FOR THE DRESSING:
1 tablespoon sherry vinegar or 1–1½ tablespoons raspberry vinegar
⅛ teaspoon salt
Freshly ground pepper
4–5 tablespoons (2–2½ fl oz/60–75 ml) extra-virgin olive oil

Separate the leaves from the heads of escarole, discarding any old or damaged leaves and the core. Rinse and dry well. Tear the leaves into small pieces and place in a bowl, cover with plastic wrap and chill to crisp for 30–40 minutes.
Cut the bacon crosswise into pieces ½ inch (12 mm) wide. Place in a heavy frying pan over medium heat and fry, stirring and tossing, until lightly browned, 3–4 minutes. Using a slotted spoon, transfer to paper towels to drain. Pour off the fat from the pan, wipe clean with a paper towel and set aside.
To make the dressing, in a small bowl, combine the vinegar, salt, and pepper to taste and stir until the salt dissolves. Gradually add 4 tablespoons (2 fl oz/60 ml) olive oil, whisking until well blended. Add another 1 tablespoon olive oil if needed to balance the flavors of the dressing. Taste and adjust the seasonings.
Remove the escarole from the refrigerator and spoon the dressing over the top. Toss until the leaves are evenly coated. Return the bacon to the reserved pan and place over medium heat to warm.
Divide the escarole among 4 plates and sprinkle with the warm bacon pieces. Serve at once.

SERVES 4

MANGO AND MELON SALAD

1 red bell pepper (capsicum)
½ cup (2 oz/60 g) walnut pieces, coarsely chopped
1 head romaine (cos) lettuce
2 oranges, preferably seedless navel
2 ripe mangoes

FOR THE DRESSING:
2 tablespoons walnut white wine vinegar
⅛ teaspoon salt
Freshly ground pepper
⅓ cup (3 fl oz/80 ml) extra-virgin olive oil

½ ripe cantaloupe, peeled, seeded and cut into 1-inch (2.5-cm) cubes
2 green (spring) onions, including some tender green tops, chopped
2 tablespoons chopped fresh mint, plus mint sprigs for garnish
12–16 Niçoise olives or Italian or Spanish black olives

Roast, peel and seed the bell pepper (see glossary, page 126). Cut lengthwise
into strips ¼ inch (6 mm) wide. Set aside.

Position a rack in the middle of an oven and preheat to 325°F (165°C).
Spread the walnuts on a baking sheet. Place in the oven and bake until they
begin to change color and are fragrant, 6–8 minutes. Set aside to cool.

Separate the lettuce leaves, discarding any old or damaged leaves and the core.
Rinse carefully and dry well. Set aside 8 good leaves for garnishing and tear the
other leaves into bite-sized pieces. Place in a large bowl and set aside.

Peel and section the oranges (see glossary, page 124). Set aside. Peel each mango,
then slice off the flesh in one piece from each side of the flat pit. Cut into 1-inch
(2.5-cm) pieces. Slice the flesh from around the pit edges as well. Set aside.

To make the dressing, in a small bowl, combine the walnut vinegar, salt, and
pepper to taste and stir until the salt dissolves. Gradually add the olive oil, whisking until well blended. Taste and adjust the seasonings.

To the bowl holding the lettuce, add the cantaloupe, green onions, chopped
mint, bell pepper, walnuts and mangoes. Whisk the dressing again and drizzle
over the fruit. Toss gently until well mixed.

For each salad, place 2 of the reserved lettuce leaves on opposite sides of a
plate. Spoon the fruit mixture between the leaves. Garnish each salad with 3
or 4 orange segments, 3 or 4 olives and mint sprigs. Serve at once.

SERVES 4

NOTES

The French have long been
attracted to the fruits of the tropics
and the Far East, and they use
them to great advantage in their
recipes. I think you'll be intrigued
by how well the mint, green
onion and walnut marry with the
fruits in this exotic combination.

If you cannot find walnut-infused
white wine vinegar, imported
from France, feel free to substitute
a good-quality,
mild white wine
vinegar.

Chicken and tarragon are made for each other. Tarragon is one of those herbs that can be used in abundance, and it takes a considerable amount to flavor a chicken properly. Do not be timid with it.

To roast the chicken to the ideal degree of doneness, I suggest you use an instant-read thermometer to check the temperature (see page 125). Because the thighs need to reach a higher internal temperature than the breast, the recipe calls for placing the chicken on its side for part of the roasting time. During roasting, add chicken broth to the pan as needed for basting.

Champagne grapes and tarragon sprigs make a festive garnish.

ROAST TARRAGON CHICKEN

1 roasting chicken, 4–4½ lb (2–2.25 kg), preferably free-range
½ lemon
8 large fresh tarragon sprigs, plus 1 tablespoon chopped fresh tarragon
1 large green (spring) onion, trimmed and cut in half crosswise,
    plus 2 teaspoons chopped green (spring) onion
Salt
3 tablespoons unsalted butter, at room temperature
Freshly ground pepper
1 cup (8 fl oz/250 ml) chicken broth, plus additional broth as needed
2 teaspoons all-purpose (plain) flour

Position a rack in the lower part of an oven and preheat the oven to 425°F (220°C). Grease a rack, preferably V-shaped, and place in a roasting pan.
🍗 Remove the fat from around the chicken cavity openings. Rinse the chicken inside and out and pat dry with paper towels. Firmly rub the cavity of the chicken with the lemon half, squeezing out a little of the juice as you do so. Place 6 of the tarragon sprigs in the cavity together with the halved green onion and a sprinkling of salt. Secure the cavity closed with a short metal skewer, trussing pin or sturdy toothpick. Using kitchen string, truss the chicken (see glossary, page 125). Tuck 1 tarragon sprig between each leg and the body of the chicken.
🍗 Using 2 tablespoons of the butter, butter the outside of the chicken and sprinkle with salt and pepper. Place it on its side on the greased rack. Add the 1 cup (8 fl oz/250 ml) chicken broth to the pan and roast for 20 minutes, basting occasionally. Turn the chicken onto its opposite side and roast for another 20 minutes, adding more broth if needed. Turn the chicken breast-side up, reduce the heat to 375°F (190°C) and continue to roast, basting with the pan juices every 10 minutes, until it is golden brown and tests done, 30–40 minutes longer; test for doneness as shown on page 125.
🍗 Transfer the chicken to a warmed serving platter and cover with aluminum foil. Let rest for 10–15 minutes before carving. Remove the rack and skim off the fat from the pan juices. Pour the pan juices into a glass measuring cup and add broth as needed to make 1½ cups (12 fl oz/375 ml). In a small saucepan over medium-low heat, melt the remaining 1 tablespoon butter. Add the chopped onion and sauté for 1 minute. Add the flour and cook, stirring, until bubbly, 1–2 minutes. Raise the heat to medium and gradually add the pan juices, stirring constantly. Stir until the mixture thickens and comes to a boil, 3–4 minutes. Add the chopped tarragon and season to taste with salt and pepper.
🍗 Carve the chicken and serve with a little sauce spooned on top.

SERVES 4

You'll find chicken stews like this in the Basque region of France, located near the border with Spain. The combination of tomatoes, peppers and bacon gives the dish a robust flavor. Serve it with crusty country bread to sop up the juices.

Shop for a good lean smoked bacon. The kind sliced to order from a slab by your butcher is likely to have the best flavor.

BASQUE CHICKEN STEW

1 red and 1 green bell pepper (capsicum), about 6 oz (185 g) each
2 chicken breast halves, 2 legs and 2 thighs, 2½–3 lb (1.25–1.5 kg) total weight
¼ lb (125 g) thickly sliced bacon, cut into pieces ½ inch (12 mm) wide
3 cloves garlic, chopped
1 yellow onion, ½ lb (250 g), cut into thin wedges
1 lb (500 g) small white boiling potatoes such as Yukon Gold or White Rose, peeled and cut in halves or quarters, depending upon size
1 lb (500 g) ripe tomatoes, peeled, seeded and chopped *(see glossary, page 124)*
2 or 3 fresh parsley sprigs
3 fresh thyme sprigs
1 bay leaf
1 celery stalk, cut crosswise into 4 equal pieces
1½ tablespoons all-purpose (plain) flour
½ cup (4 fl oz/125 ml) each dry white wine and chicken broth, heated
Salt, freshly ground black pepper and cayenne pepper

Roast and peel the bell peppers (see glossary, page 126). Cut into long strips ½ inch (12 mm) wide. Set aside. Remove the skin and fat from the chicken pieces; cut the breasts in half crosswise.

In a large sauté pan over medium heat, cook the bacon until golden, about 10 minutes. Using a slotted spoon, transfer to a stew pot. Reduce the heat to medium-low, add the garlic and onion and sauté until soft, 6–7 minutes. Using the slotted spoon, transfer to the stew pot. Set the pan aside. Add the potatoes, tomatoes and pepper strips to the stew pot. Place the parsley and thyme sprigs and bay leaf inside the celery pieces and tie with kitchen string; add to the pot.

Return the sauté pan to medium-high heat. Add the chicken and sauté in the bacon fat until lightly browned, 5–6 minutes on each side. Transfer to the stew pot. Pour off all but 1 tablespoon of the fat from the pan. Add the flour and stir over medium heat until blended. Cook, stirring, for 1 minute, then add the wine and broth. Continue to stir, scraping up any browned bits. Cook until thickened, 2–3 minutes. Pour over the chicken; add salt, black pepper and cayenne to taste. Cover and bring to a simmer, reduce the heat and simmer until the juices have increased, about 25 minutes. Rearrange the chicken and vegetables, re-cover and simmer until the chicken is tender, 20–25 minutes longer. The meat should be opaque throughout.

Adjust the seasonings. Discard the herb bouquet. Transfer the chicken, vegetables and sauce to a warmed serving dish and serve at once.

SERVES 4

CHICKEN WITH FENNEL

2 fennel bulbs, about 2 lb (1 kg) total weight
1 chicken, 3½–4 lb (1.75–2 kg), preferably free-range
½ yellow onion, cut into 4 wedges
2 bay leaves
Salt and freshly ground pepper
2 tablespoons unsalted butter
2 tablespoons olive oil
4 carrots, peeled and cut crosswise into slices ¼ inch (6 mm) thick
¼ cup (2 fl oz/60 ml) dry white wine

Position a rack in the lower third of an oven and preheat to 400°F (200°C).

Trim the root end and the stalks from the fennel bulbs and remove any old or bruised outer leaves. Holding the bulbs root-end down and starting on the narrow side, cut vertically into slices ¼ inch (6 mm) thick. Set aside.

Remove the giblets, if any, from the chicken cavity and put aside for another use. Remove the fat from around the cavity openings. Rinse the chicken inside and out and pat dry with paper towels.

Place the onion wedges and 1 of the bay leaves in the cavity and sprinkle the cavity with salt and pepper to taste. Secure the cavity closed with a short metal skewer, trussing pin or sturdy toothpick. Using kitchen string, truss the chicken (see glossary, page 125). Select a heavy ovenproof stew pot that will accommodate the chicken comfortably and place it over medium-high heat. Add the butter and olive oil. When foaming, add the chicken and lightly brown on all sides, 10–12 minutes. Transfer to a plate.

Pour off the fat and wipe out the pot with paper towels. Place the remaining bay leaf, fennel and carrots in a layer on the pot bottom. Place the chicken, breast-side down, on the vegetables. Sprinkle with salt and pepper and pour in the wine. Cover and roast for 30 minutes. Turn the chicken breast-side up, cover and continue to roast until tender, 20–30 minutes longer. To test for doneness, insert an instant-read thermometer in the thickest part of the breast or the thigh without touching the bone; it should register 165°F (74°C) in the breast or 180°F (82°C) in the thigh. Or pierce the thigh joint with the tip of a knife; the juices should run clear. Set aside with the cover ajar for 5–10 minutes.

Transfer the chicken to a warmed deep serving platter and carve. Using a slotted spoon, transfer the vegetables to the platter, arranging them around the chicken. Using a large spoon, skim off any fat from the pot juices. Taste the juices and adjust the seasonings. Spoon them over the chicken and serve.

SERVES 4

NOTES

Most of the best meals in France are built around a slowly cooked, well-seasoned dish. This pot-roasted chicken is one of them. Try making this on a Sunday, when you have a little more time. You'll no doubt enjoy the leftovers for a weeknight meal.

Fennel, I have found, is one of the best vegetables to cook with chicken. This is especially so when you slowly roast the bird in a pot, as the extended cooking allows the vegetable's mild anise flavor to be absorbed by the meat.

CHICKEN BREASTS WITH MUSTARD SAUCE

I recommend serving this simple chicken sauté with freshly cooked asparagus or peas. To begin the meal, serve Asparagus with Orange Hollandaise Sauce (recipe on page 6) or the Mango and Melon Salad (page 43) and perhaps finish with a fruit tart.

The key to this recipe's success comes in flattening the chicken breasts to an even thickness before cooking them. They will cook evenly and stay perfectly moist throughout.

4 chicken breast halves, 8–9 oz (250–280 g) each, skinned and boned
  (5–6 oz/155–185 g when boned)
1 tablespoon unsalted butter
1 tablespoon vegetable oil
Salt and freshly ground pepper
3 tablespoons chopped shallots (2 or 3 shallots)
2 tablespoons Dijon-style mustard
½ cup (4 fl oz/125 ml) heavy (double) cream
Chopped fresh parsley

Trim any fat from the chicken breasts. Rinse and pat dry with paper towels. One at a time, place each chicken breast between 2 sheets of waxed paper or plastic wrap and, using a rolling pin, roll across the thickest part of the breast to flatten to an even thickness of about ½ inch (12 mm).

In a large, preferably nonstick sauté pan or frying pan over medium-high heat, melt the butter with the oil. When foaming, add the chicken breasts and sprinkle with salt and pepper to taste. Sauté, adjusting the heat as needed to keep the breasts from releasing their juices, until golden and just tender, about 5 minutes on each side. To test for doneness, insert the tip of a sharp knife into the center of a breast; the juices should run clear and the meat should no longer be pink at the center. Transfer to a warmed plate and keep warm.

Pour off any excess fat from the pan and return the pan to medium-low heat. Add the shallots and sauté, stirring, until translucent, 1–2 minutes. Add the mustard and cream, raise the heat to medium and stir with a wooden spoon, scraping up any browned bits stuck to the pan bottom. Cook, stirring, until thickened and blended, 2–3 minutes. Taste and adjust the seasonings.

Return the chicken breasts to the pan and turn the breasts over several times to coat them well with the sauce and to heat them through. Transfer to a warmed platter or individual plates and spoon the sauce over the breasts. Sprinkle with chopped parsley and serve at once.

SERVES 4

CHICKEN AND SWEET POTATO

1 chicken, 3½–4 lb (1.75–2 kg), cut into serving pieces
3 tablespoons unsalted butter
2 tablespoons vegetable oil
2 or 3 sweet potatoes, 1½–2 lb (750 g–1 kg) total weight, peeled and
    cut crosswise into slices ½ inch (12 mm) thick
8–10 shallots, cut crosswise into slices ⅛ inch (3 mm) thick
½ cup (4 fl oz/125 ml) pure apple juice, plus additional juice as needed
½ cup (4 fl oz/125 ml) chicken broth, plus additional broth as needed
6–8 fresh sage leaves, plus 2 or 3 fresh sage sprigs for garnish
Salt and freshly ground pepper
1 tablespoon all-purpose (plain) flour
¼ cup (2 fl oz/60 ml) heavy (double) cream

Position a rack in the middle of an oven and preheat to 375°F (190°C). Butter a large baking dish or pan that will hold the chicken and potatoes in a single layer.
🍶 Cut the 2 chicken breast halves in half crosswise. Cut the thighs and legs apart. Remove the wing tips and save along with the back for another use. You should have 10 pieces. Remove any fat from them. Rinse and pat dry with paper towels.
🍶 In a sauté pan over medium-high heat, melt 2 tablespoons of the butter with the oil. When foaming, add half of the chicken and quickly sear until golden, 4–5 minutes on each side. Transfer to the prepared dish. Repeat with the remaining chicken. Arrange the potato slices among the chicken pieces.
🍶 Reduce the heat to medium-low and add the shallots. Sauté until translucent, 2–3 minutes. Add half each of the apple juice and broth and stir, scraping up any browned bits. Bring to a boil and pour over the chicken and potatoes. Tuck the 6–8 sage leaves around the chicken. Sprinkle with salt and pepper.
🍶 Bake until the potatoes and chicken are tender, 45–50 minutes. The meat should be opaque throughout. Using a slotted spoon, transfer the chicken and potatoes to a warmed serving dish and cover to keep warm. Using a large spoon, skim off the fat from the juices and pour the juices into a pitcher.
🍶 In a small saucepan over medium-low heat, melt the remaining 1 tablespoon butter. Add the flour and cook, stirring, until bubbly, 1–2 minutes. Raise the heat to medium. Stirring constantly, gradually add the remaining ¼ cup (2 fl oz/ 60 ml) each apple juice and broth and the pan juices. Stir until the mixture thickens and comes to a boil, 3–4 minutes. Add the cream and cook for a few seconds. Thin, if desired, with apple juice or broth; adjust the seasonings. Pour the sauce over the chicken and potatoes. Garnish with sage sprigs and serve.

SERVES 4

NOTES

Yes, the French do like sweet potatoes. This is a dish you are apt to find in a small country hotel in the northwestern province of Normandy. They would probably use the region's familiar apple brandy, Calvados, rather than the apple juice I call for in this recipe. If you like, you can add 1 or 2 tablespoons Calvados to the dish. Look for apple juice labeled "pure"; avoid those made from apple concentrate.

Do not use dried sage. The fresh leaves have a much better flavor and are worth seeking out in a well-stocked market.

CHICKEN WITH BASIL AIOLI

Although you might not think so at first, it is just as important to guard against overcooking a chicken when poaching as when roasting or sautéing it. Be careful not to let the liquid boil; maintain a very gentle simmer with only a few bubbles rising to the surface. As the poaching progresses, I usually find it necessary to reduce the heat slightly.

Basil aioli is an herbed variation on the French garlic mayonnaise known as aioli, made here with fresh basil and less garlic. It is a lovely accompaniment to the mild, tender poultry.

Save the cooking broth for another meal. Serve it as a clear soup, or add vegetables and chicken pieces for a more hearty soup. The broth can be refrigerated for several days.

1 chicken, 3½–4 lb (1.75–2 kg), preferably free-range
1 small yellow onion, quartered
1 celery stalk, cut into 2-inch (5-cm) lengths
3 fresh thyme sprigs
3 fresh parsley sprigs, plus chopped parsley for garnish
1 bay leaf
1 large lemon wedge
8 cups (64 fl oz/2 l) chicken broth, heated almost to boiling
Basil Aioli *(recipe on page 118)*
1½ lb (750 g) leeks (about 4 leeks), trimmed and cleaned *(see glossary, page 125)*
6 carrots, peeled, cut in half crosswise and top section cut in half lengthwise
Salt and freshly ground pepper

Remove the neck and giblets, if any, from the chicken cavity; set aside. Remove the fat from around the cavity openings. Rinse inside and out and pat dry with paper towels. Place the onion, celery, thyme and parsley sprigs, bay leaf and lemon wedge in the cavity. Close the cavity with a short metal skewer, trussing pin or sturdy toothpick. Using kitchen string, truss the chicken (see glossary, page 125). Place breast-side up in a deep pot in which it just fits. Add the neck and giblets as well, if included. Pour in the broth. If the liquid does not reach three-fourths of the way up the sides of the chicken, add hot water as needed. Place over high heat and bring just under a boil. Using a skimmer, remove any scum as it rises to the surface. Reduce the heat to medium-low or low, cover and cook at a bare simmer for 30 minutes. Meanwhile, make the Basil Aioli.

🍶 Turn the chicken breast-side down and add the leeks, carrots, and salt and pepper to taste. Continue to simmer until tender, another 35–50 minutes. To test for doneness, insert an instant-read thermometer in the thickest part of the thigh without touching the bone; it should register 180°F (82°C). Or turn breast-side up and test the breast; it should register 165°F (74°C). Alternatively, pierce the thigh joint with a knife tip; the juices should run clear.

🍶 Transfer the chicken to a warmed platter and cover loosely with aluminum foil. Let rest for 10 minutes. Continue to cook the vegetables until tender, if necessary. Then, using a slotted spoon, transfer the vegetables to the platter.

🍶 Carve the chicken and serve on warmed plates with the vegetables. Make sure that the chicken and vegetables are thoroughly moistened with the cooking liquid. Garnish with chopped parsley. Spoon the aioli over the chicken or pass it in a bowl.

SERVES 4

CHICKEN WITH COUSCOUS

2 red bell peppers (capsicums)
1 bunch leeks, 1–1½ lb (500–750 g)
1 chicken, 3½–4 lb (1.75–2 kg), preferably free-range, cut into serving pieces
3 tablespoons unsalted butter
2 tablespoons olive oil
2 large cloves garlic, thinly sliced
½ cup (4 fl oz/125 ml) chicken broth, plus additional broth as needed
1 bay leaf
3 fresh thyme sprigs
Salt and freshly ground pepper
1 tablespoon all-purpose (plain) flour
Couscous *(recipe on page 118)*
Chopped fresh parsley

Roast and peel the peppers (see glossary, page 126). Cut into long strips
¼ inch (6 mm) wide. Trim and rinse the leeks, leaving 1 inch (2.5 cm) of the
greens (see glossary, page 125). Slice crosswise ½ inch (12 mm) thick. Set aside.
Cut the 2 chicken breast halves in half crosswise. Cut the thighs and legs apart.
Remove the wing tips and save along with the back for another use. You should
have 10 pieces. Remove any fat. Rinse and pat dry with paper towels.
In a Dutch oven over medium-high heat, melt 2 tablespoons of the butter
with the olive oil. Add half of the chicken and brown lightly, 4–5 minutes on
each side. Transfer to a plate. Repeat with the remaining chicken.
Pour off most of the fat from the pot and place over low heat. Add the garlic
and sauté until it begins to change color, 30–40 seconds. Add the leeks and sauté
until they begin to wilt, 3–4 minutes. Add the ½ cup (4 fl oz/125 ml) broth and
stir, scraping up any browned bits. Return the chicken pieces to the pot, in a
single layer, over the leeks. Tuck the bay leaf and thyme sprigs under the chicken.
Cover and barely simmer for 40 minutes. Add the pepper strips and salt and
pepper to taste and simmer until the chicken is opaque throughout when
pierced with a knife, another 30–45 minutes.
Transfer the chicken and leeks to a plate. Skim off the fat from the pot juices.
Transfer the juices to a measuring cup and add chicken broth to make 1½ cups
(12 fl oz/375 ml). Add the remaining 1 tablespoon butter to the pot and return
to medium heat. When foaming, add the flour and cook, stirring, until bubbly,
2–3 minutes. Gradually add the pot juices, stirring constantly until thickened and
boiling, 3–4 minutes. Return the chicken and leeks to the pot; keep warm.
Make the couscous and spoon onto a warmed platter. Surround with the
chicken and leeks, sprinkle with chopped parsley and serve.

SERVES 4

NOTES

A holdover from France's colonial
years in North Africa, couscous
has been adopted by the French as
a grain that rivals rice in popu-
larity. I find that it makes a great
accompaniment to stews, braises
and other dishes that have an
abundance of sauce.

Quick-cooking varieties of
packaged couscous produce satis-
factory results, and are far more
convenient to cook than rice.
Take care to read the cooking
instructions on the package, as
products can vary from one
manufacturer to another.

This recipe is easy to put together,
and much of the preparation can
be done in advance. For a weekend dinner, accompany it with
a salad and a fruit dessert.

Quickly cooked fish fillets and mushrooms topped with a buttery hollandaise is one of the most venerable dishes of French cuisine. Other firm white fish fillets such as sea bass or swordfish may be substituted.

If you have never made a hollandaise sauce before, I urge you to try it. You'll be surprised how easy it is to make (see my pointers in the note on page 6), and it truly does turn a plain dish into a special one. I prefer to use a bowl over simmering water rather than a double boiler for hollandaise. The sauce is easier to whisk and absorbs heat more slowly.

HALIBUT WITH HOLLANDAISE

2 tablespoons chopped shallots (about 2 shallots)
½ lb (250 g) small, firm fresh mushrooms
4 halibut fillets, 6–7 oz (185–220 g) each and about 1 inch (2.5 cm) thick
¼ cup (2 fl oz/60 ml) dry white wine
Salt and freshly ground pepper

FOR THE HOLLANDAISE SAUCE:
3 egg yolks, at room temperature
1½ tablespoons fresh lemon juice, plus extra if needed
¾ cup (6 oz/185 g) unsalted butter, cut into slices ¼ inch
   (6 mm) thick, at room temperature

Chopped fresh parsley

Position a rack in the middle of an oven and preheat to 425°F (220°C). Butter a flameproof rectangular or oval baking dish that will accommodate the fish fillets comfortably in a single layer. Sprinkle the shallots evenly over the bottom.

Brush off any dirt from the mushrooms. Do not rinse in water. Cut into slices ¼ inch (6 mm) thick and spread over the shallots.

Rinse the halibut and pat dry with paper towels. Lay the fillets over the mushrooms and pour in the wine. Season to taste with salt and pepper. Cover and bake until opaque throughout when pierced with a sharp knife, 10–15 minutes.

Meanwhile, make the hollandaise: Place the egg yolks and 1½ tablespoons lemon juice in a heatproof bowl or the top pan of a double boiler. Set over (but not touching) barely simmering water in a saucepan or the bottom pan of the double boiler. Whisk until beginning to thicken, about 1 minute. Whisk in the butter, 1 slice at a time. Continue to whisk until thickened, 2–3 minutes; do not overcook. Remove from the pan of hot water and continue whisking until cooled slightly. Cover partially and keep warm. Do not discard the hot water.

When the fillets test done, carefully drain off the liquid from the dish into a small saucepan. Cover the dish to keep the fillets warm. Place the saucepan over high heat and boil until the liquid is reduced by about half, 2–3 minutes.

Preheat a broiler (griller). Reposition the hollandaise over the simmering water. Whisk in the reduced liquid, 1 tablespoon at a time, until thinned slightly; it will take no more than 2–3 tablespoons. Season to taste with salt and pepper and more lemon juice, if needed. Again drain off any liquid that has accumulated in the baking dish, then spoon the sauce over the fillets. Broil (grill) until lightly browned, 1–2 minutes. Sprinkle with parsley and serve immediately.

SERVES 4

STEAMED MUSSELS

NOTES

3½–4 lb (1.75–2 kg) mussels, preferably medium
¼ cup (2 oz/60 g) unsalted butter
¼ cup (1¼ oz/37 g) minced shallots (about 4 shallots)
1 small bay leaf
1 tablespoon chopped fresh thyme
1 cup (8 fl oz/250 ml) dry white wine
6 tablespoons chopped fresh parsley
Salt and freshly ground pepper
Crusty French bread

Scrub the mussels thoroughly under running water, removing any beards clinging to the shells. Discard any mussels that do not close to the touch.

In a large pot over medium-low heat, melt the butter. When foaming, add the shallots and sauté, stirring, until translucent, 2–3 minutes. Add the bay leaf, thyme and wine, raise the heat to medium-high and cook for about 2 minutes. Add the mussels, sprinkle 4 tablespoons of the parsley over the mussels and sprinkle to taste with salt and pepper. Cover and steam, shaking the pan to toss about the mussels once or twice, until the mussels open, about 5 minutes.

Using a slotted spoon, transfer the mussels to 4 warmed soup plates or bowls, dividing them equally. Discard any mussels that have not opened. Spoon the broth over the mussels and sprinkle with the remaining 2 tablespoons chopped parsley. Serve with crusty French bread to sop up the juices, and provide small bowls at the table for discarding the shells.

SERVES 4

On my many midwinter trips to Paris during the 1960s tracking down kitchenware for the first Williams-Sonoma shop, I always looked forward to a Metro ride out to the flea market on a Saturday, which meant I would have steamed mussels—*moules marinières*—at Chez Louisette, a small, popular restaurant in one of the market alleyways. The hot, aromatic bowlful of shellfish, served with crusty bread to soak up the juices, brought me absolute bliss.

I have never forgotten this dish, and have never tasted mussels as good—that is, until developing, testing and writing this recipe took me back to the sixties.

GRILLED SWORDFISH WITH TOMATO SAUCE

2 lb (1 kg) ripe tomatoes
5 tablespoons (2½ fl oz/75 ml) olive oil
2 tablespoons chopped garlic (6 or 7 cloves)
1 yellow onion, chopped (about 1 cup/5 oz/155 g)
¼ cup (2 fl oz/60 ml) red wine
Salt and freshly ground pepper
3 tablespoons chopped fresh basil, plus whole leaves for garnish
4 swordfish steaks, 7–8 oz (220–250 g) each and 1 inch (2.5 cm) thick

Prepare a fire in a charcoal grill. Place the grill rack 4–6 inches (10–15 cm) above the heat and brush it with oil.

To make the sauce, core, peel and seed the tomatoes (see glossary, page 124). Chop coarsely; you should have about 4 cups (1½ lb/750 g). In a saucepan over medium-low heat, warm 2 tablespoons of the olive oil. When hot but not smoking, add 1 tablespoon of the garlic and sauté, stirring, until it begins to change color, 30–40 seconds. Add the onion and continue to sauté, stirring occasionally, until translucent, 6–7 minutes. Raise the heat to medium, add the tomatoes and cook, stirring, until they release some of their liquid, 6–7 minutes. Add the wine, reduce the heat to medium-low and simmer until the liquid is reduced by half, 8–10 minutes. Remove from the heat and let cool slightly.

While the sauce is cooking, place the swordfish steaks in a large dish in a single layer. In a small bowl, combine the remaining 3 tablespoons oil, 1 tablespoon garlic, 1 tablespoon basil and a little salt and pepper. Stir well and brush on both sides of the fish steaks. Set aside for about 10 minutes.

Transfer the tomato mixture to a food processor fitted with the metal blade or to a blender and process, using a few pulses, to produce a coarse purée. Return the sauce to the saucepan and season to taste with salt and pepper. Stir in the remaining 2 tablespoons basil and return the pan to medium-low heat. Cook for a few minutes to blend the flavors, then taste and adjust the seasonings. Remove from the heat, set aside and keep warm.

When the fire is ready, grill the fish, turning once or twice, until opaque throughout when pierced with a knife tip, 10–12 minutes total.

If the sauce has cooled, reheat it over medium-low heat. Place 3–4 spoonfuls of sauce on each warmed plate to make a bed for the fish. Place a swordfish steak on each bed of sauce and garnish with basil leaves. Serve at once.

SERVES 4

Curried Shrimp with Rice

1 large mango
2 or 3 green (spring) onions, including some tender green tops, coarsely chopped
Leaves from 2 or 3 fresh cilantro (fresh coriander) sprigs, coarsely chopped
1 lime
Cayenne pepper
1½ lb (750 g) small or medium fresh shrimp (prawns), peeled and deveined
Salt
1¾ cups (14 fl oz/440 ml) water
2 cups (14 oz/440 g) jasmine rice or other long-grain white rice, rinsed
2 tablespoons unsalted butter
1 tablespoon olive oil
1 or 2 garlic cloves, peeled and finely chopped
1 white sweet onion, chopped (about 1 cup/5 oz/155 g)
1½ tablespoons curry powder
¾ cup (6 fl oz/180 ml) dry white wine
1 cup (8 fl oz/250 ml) coconut milk

Peel the mango, then slice off the flesh in one piece from each side of the flat pit. Cut into ½-inch (12-mm) cubes. Slice the flesh from the edges of the pit as well. Place in a small bowl and add the green onions and cilantro. Remove the zest from the lime (see glossary, page 126), shredding it directly over the mango. Cut the lime in half and squeeze the juice from one half over the fruit. Add a dash of cayenne, toss and adjust the seasonings. Set aside.

Put the shrimp in a bowl with water to cover. Add 1 teaspoon salt, stir to dissolve and let stand for 10 minutes. Drain, rinse and drain again. Set aside.

In a saucepan, bring the water to a boil. Add the rice and ¼ teaspoon salt and stir twice. Reduce the heat to low, cover and cook until the water is absorbed, about 20 minutes. Let stand, covered, for 10 minutes off the heat.

Meanwhile, in a sauté pan over medium-low heat, melt the butter with the oil. Add the garlic and sauté for a few seconds. Add the onion and sauté until translucent, 4–5 minutes. Add the curry powder, stir and sauté for 1 minute. Raise the heat to medium, add the wine and cook until the onion is tender and the liquid is reduced by one-third, 8–10 minutes. Add the coconut milk, bring to a simmer and add the shrimp. Reduce the heat to low, cover and cook until the shrimp are red and opaque, 2–3 minutes. Season with salt, cayenne and lime juice.

Spoon the rice onto the center of warmed plates. Place the shrimp mixture along one side and the mango relish along the other, then serve.

Serves 4

NOTES

The French love of exotic seasonings and fruits, which dates back to their colonial era, is evident in this Parisian bistro recipe. The relish, a combination of fresh mango, green onion, cilantro and lime, perfectly balances the aromatic flavors of the curried shrimp.

Be sure to use fresh curry powder. If a container has been sitting in your cupboard for more than six months, it probably has lost much of its punch. Buy a fresh supply from a source that is likely to have a good turnover of the product, such as an ethnic market. Tins of coconut milk and bags or boxes of jasmine rice, a fragrant long-grain white rice grown in Thailand, can also be purchased at ethnic markets, as well as in specialty-food shops and the international section of many large food stores.

FILLETS OF SOLE WITH GRAPES

NOTES

An elegant classic of French cooking, this is probably one of the easiest dishes to prepare at the last minute. The secret to success lies in having everything laid out before the cooking begins. Bear in mind, too, that the dish is finished under the broiler, so take care not to overcook the fish fillets when sautéing them.

Other thin white fish fillets such as red snapper or sand dab can be used in place of the sole. Make sure that the grapes you select are sweet; sometimes grapes are picked too soon and can be on the sour side.

4 sole fillets, 6–7 oz (185–220 g) each
½ cup (2½ oz/75 g) all-purpose (plain) flour
Salt and freshly ground pepper
3 tablespoons unsalted butter
1 tablespoon olive oil or vegetable oil
¼ cup (1¼ oz/37 g) chopped shallots (about 4 shallots)
¾ cup (6 fl oz/180 ml) dry white wine or white vermouth
1½ cups (9 oz/280 g) white seedless grapes
Fresh dill sprigs

Preheat a broiler (griller).

🐟 Rinse the fish fillets and pat dry with paper towels. Place the flour, ¼ teaspoon salt and ⅛ teaspoon pepper on a plate and mix together. Lightly dredge the fillets in the flour mixture, coating evenly on both sides and shaking off the excess.

🐟 In a large sauté pan or frying pan over medium-high heat, melt the butter with the oil. When foaming, add the fillets, in 2 batches if necessary to prevent crowding, and sauté, turning once, until starting to turn golden, about 2 minutes on each side. Using a slotted spatula, transfer the fillets to a warmed flameproof baking dish that will hold them in a single layer; keep warm.

🐟 Add the shallots to the same pan, reduce the heat to low and sauté, stirring, until translucent, 1–2 minutes. Pour off any excess fat, but reserve the shallots in the pan. Add the wine and bring to a boil over medium-high heat. Boil until reduced by about one-third, scraping up any browned bits on the pan bottom. Add the grapes and continue to boil until the liquid is reduced a little more, 1–2 minutes. Season to taste with salt and pepper and pour over the fillets, distributing the grapes and shallots evenly over and around the fish pieces.

🐟 Place under the broiler, with the top of the fillets about 4 inches (10 cm) from the heat source. Broil (grill) until the top is just beginning to brown and the sauce is bubbly, 2–3 minutes. Garnish with dill sprigs and serve immediately.

SERVES 4

FISH STEW WITH COUSCOUS

NOTES

While I love the classic bouilla-baisse, it can be time-consuming to make. I have found that some of France's simpler fish stews, such as this one borrowed from Algiers, are exceptionally good.

Frozen fish stock, now available at better food markets, can be excellent; do take advantage of it. If you cannot find an acceptable product and do not care to make stock yourself, feel free to substitute bottled clam juice.

Because I prefer the taste and texture of dried chick-peas, I make sure to cook them well in advance. If time is a problem, though, you can use canned ones. You will need 1 cup (7 oz/220 g). Rinse them before adding to the stew.

½ cup (3½ oz/105 g) dried chick-peas (garbanzo beans)
1 lb (500 g) ripe plum (Roma) tomatoes
2 tablespoons olive oil
1 tablespoon minced garlic (2 or 3 cloves)
1 white sweet onion, chopped (¾–1 cup/4–5 oz/125–155 g)
1 cup (4 oz/125 g) thinly sliced carrot (2 or 3 carrots)
1 cup (4 oz/125 g) thinly sliced celery (about 3 stalks)
1½ teaspoons ground turmeric
2 teaspoons ground cumin
⅛ teaspoon red pepper flakes
Pinch of ground cloves
2 cups (16 fl oz/500 ml) fish stock *(see notes)*
1 cup (8 fl oz/250 ml) water
2 zucchini (courgettes), cut crosswise into slices ¼ inch (6 mm) thick
½ cup (3 oz/90 g) golden raisins (sultanas)
Salt and freshly ground pepper
2 lb (1 kg) assorted white fish fillets such as sea bass, halibut and snapper
Couscous *(recipe on page 118)*

Sort through the chick-peas, discarding any damaged peas or small stones. Rinse and drain. Place in a saucepan and add water to cover by 2 inches (5 cm). Bring to a boil, remove from the heat, cover and let soak for 1 hour. Drain, rinse and return to the pan. Again add water to cover by 2 inches (5 cm). Bring to a boil, reduce the heat to low, cover and simmer until tender, about 1 hour. Drain.

Core, peel and seed the tomatoes (see glossary, page 124). Chop coarsely.

In a large sauté pan over medium-low heat, warm the oil. When hot, add the garlic and sauté until it begins to change color, 30–40 seconds. Add the onion and sauté until translucent, 6–7 minutes. Add the chick-peas, tomatoes, carrot, celery, turmeric, cumin, red pepper flakes, cloves, fish stock and water. Cover partially and simmer until barely tender, 20–25 minutes. Add the zucchini, raisins, and salt and pepper to taste and simmer for 6–7 minutes longer. Adjust the seasonings.

Rinse the fish and cut into pieces 1 inch (2.5 cm) by 1½ inches (4 cm). Add to the stew, immersing them in the liquid. Cover and cook over very low heat until the fish is opaque throughout when pierced with a knife tip, 10–15 minutes.

About 15 minutes before serving, prepare the couscous and have ready.

Spoon the couscous into warmed deep plates and spoon the stew around it. Serve immediately.

SERVES 4

BAKED SALMON FILLET WITH SPINACH

1 bunch spinach, about 1 lb (500 g)
3 tablespoons unsalted butter
2 tablespoons minced green (spring) onion, including some
  tender green tops (2 or 3 onions)
Salt and freshly ground pepper
Freshly grated nutmeg
1 tail end piece salmon, about 2 lb (1 kg), skinned and boned *(see notes)*
1 lemon
Chopped fresh parsley
Parsley sprigs, dill sprigs or green onions for garnish

Position a rack in the center of an oven and preheat to 425°F (220°C). Butter the bottom of a rectangular or oval baking dish that will hold the salmon comfortably.

Remove the stems from the spinach and discard. Discard any old or bruised leaves. Rinse the spinach thoroughly and place in a large saucepan with just the water clinging to the leaves. Cover and place over medium heat. Cook, turning once or twice, just until the leaves are wilted, about 2 minutes. Transfer to a colander and drain, pressing out any excess water with a large spoon. Fluff up with a fork, place on a clean cutting surface and, using a sharp knife, chop finely. Set aside.

In a small saucepan over medium-low heat, melt 2 tablespoons of the butter. Add the green onion and sauté gently, stirring, until translucent, 1–2 minutes. Add the spinach and stir to incorporate. Season to taste with salt, pepper and nutmeg. Remove from the heat and set aside.

Rinse the salmon tail piece, then pat dry with paper towels. You should have 2 matching fillets.

Lay 1 salmon fillet in the baking dish, skinned side down. Arrange the spinach evenly on top. Place the other fillet on top, skinned side up. Cut the remaining 1 tablespoon butter into small pieces and dot the top of the salmon with them. Sprinkle to taste with salt and pepper. Bake until the salmon is opaque through-out when pierced with the tip of a sharp knife, about 20 minutes.

Using a spatula, transfer the salmon to a warmed serving plate. Cut the lemon into 4 or 5 thin slices and arrange them in a row down the center of the salmon. Sprinkle with chopped parsley. Garnish the plate with parsley sprigs, dill sprigs or green onions. To serve, cut the salmon into 4 equal pieces and transfer to warmed plates.

SERVES 4

NOTES

Salmon lends itself very well to baking, especially when fillets are layered with vegetables that flavor the fish while keeping it moist. Either of the hollandaise sauces on pages 6 and 58 will marry well with this dish. Any leftover salmon makes an excellent cold salad.

For this recipe, order the very end of the tail section of salmon from your fishmonger. This is the section between the cavity opening and the tail that only has the central bone structure, eliminating any chance of stray bones in the flesh. It yields two halves that are perfect for layering with the filling. Ask your fishmonger to fillet and skin the salmon for you.

Rack of Lamb with Flageolet Beans

Notes

Sweet-tasting lamb and earthy flageolet beans seem a perfect pairing, and the combination is even more appealing for the ease with which it is prepared. Instead of the usual leg of lamb, I have substituted racks of lamb, which make the dish easier still. All you need to complete the meal is a salad and a simple dessert.

The best choice of meat is the center section of the rack, which usually consists of six chops. You will need two such racks.

Dried flageolet beans may be found in specialty-food shops and in the international section of some large food stores. Now being grown in America, they are becoming more widely available. Be sure to look for small, young beans without shriveled skins. Those from a new harvest cook quickly, while older beans take longer to cook. The beans can be prepared in advance.

1 cup (7 oz/220 g) dried flageolet beans
½ yellow onion, diced (½ cup/2 oz/60 g)
1 carrot, peeled and diced (½ cup/2½ oz/75 g)
Salt
2 fresh parsley sprigs
2 fresh thyme sprigs
1 bay leaf
1 celery stalk, cut into 2-inch (5-cm) lengths
2 racks of lamb, 6 ribs each, trimmed of any fat
1 clove garlic, cut in half
2 tablespoons chopped fresh rosemary
Freshly ground pepper
2 tablespoons chopped fresh mint

Sort through the beans, discarding any damaged beans or small stones. Rinse and drain. Place in a saucepan and add water to cover by 2 inches (5 cm). Bring to a boil, remove from the heat, cover and let soak for 1 hour.

Drain, rinse and return the beans to the pan with water to cover by 1 inch (2.5 cm). Add the onion, carrot and 1 teaspoon salt. Gather the parsley and thyme sprigs and bay leaf together, enclose inside the celery pieces and tie securely to form a bouquet garni. Add to the pan, pushing it down into the beans. Bring to a boil, reduce the heat to medium-low, cover partially and simmer until the beans are tender, 30–45 minutes. Remove and discard the herb bouquet and set the pan aside.

Position an oven rack in the center of an oven and preheat to 450°F (230°C). Rub the lamb racks with the garlic halves and coat with the rosemary. Sprinkle with salt and pepper. Place on a flat baking rack, fat side down, in a roasting pan. Roast for 15 minutes. Turn fat-side up, reduce the heat to 400°F (200°C) and roast until the meat springs back to the touch, 20–30 minutes. To test, insert an instant-read thermometer into the thickest part of the meat without touching the bone; it should register 125°F (52°C) and be medium pink inside.

Meanwhile, pour off all but about ¼ cup (2 fl oz/60 ml) liquid from the beans. Return the pan to medium heat; add the mint and salt and pepper to taste. Mix gently, then simmer for a few minutes to blend the flavor. Adjust the seasonings.

Transfer the lamb to a warmed platter and cut into chops. Divide the beans among 4 warmed plates and place 3 chops on each plate. Spoon the juices from the platter over the beans. Serve at once.

Serves 4

COUNTRY VEAL STEW

NOTES

Blanquette de veau, a pale white veal stew, is one of the classic dishes of French provincial cuisine, but richer brown stews are also made with veal. This variation is the best of both. Lightly seared veal is cooked with tomatoes, garlic, onions and carrots, and the stew is given a final flavor enhancement of fresh sage and lemon juice. For the tenderest results, take special care to sear the veal pieces quickly and lightly, and to maintain the barest simmer during cooking.

If the carrots in your market are large and thick, cut them in half lengthwise before cutting them crosswise. Have your butcher cut the veal into strips as indicated, or do it yourself. Strips of this size will yield better texture and flavor than smaller pieces.

Serve the stew over rice, couscous (recipe on page 118) or noodles.

3 fresh parsley sprigs
2 fresh thyme sprigs
1 bay leaf
1 celery stalk, cut crosswise into 4 equal pieces
½ cup (2½ oz/75 g) all-purpose (plain) flour
Salt and freshly ground pepper
2 lb (1 kg) boneless shoulder of veal, trimmed of any fat and cut into strips
  2½ inches (6 cm) long, 1 inch (2.5 cm) wide and ¾ inch (2 cm) thick
2 tablespoons unsalted butter
1 tablespoon vegetable oil
3 cloves garlic, thinly sliced
½ cup (4 fl oz/125 ml) each dry white wine and water
24 small boiling onions (about 1 lb/500 g), about 1 inch (2.5 cm) in diameter
1 lb (500 g) ripe tomatoes, peeled, seeded and finely diced *(see glossary, page 124)*
1 bunch small carrots, peeled and cut on the diagonal into 2-inch (5-cm) lengths
1 tablespoon cornstarch mixed with 2 tablespoons water, optional
4 fresh sage leaves, coarsely chopped, plus chopped sage and parsley for garnish
1 lemon, cut in half

Place the parsley and thyme sprigs and bay leaf inside the celery pieces and tie with kitchen string. Set aside. Mix the flour, ¾ teaspoon salt and ⅛ teaspoon pepper on a plate. Lightly coat the veal pieces with the mixture.

In a large sauté pan over medium-high heat, melt the butter with the oil. Add the veal and quickly sear, 3–4 minutes on each side. Transfer to a plate. Pour off any fat and reduce the heat to medium-low. Add the garlic and sauté for 30–40 seconds. Add the wine and water and raise the heat to medium. Simmer, scraping up any browned bits. Return the meat to the pan, add the herb bouquet, reduce the heat to low, partially cover and barely simmer until almost tender, about 1 hour.

Meanwhile, bring a saucepan of water to a boil, add the onions and boil for 3 minutes. Drain and immerse in cold water. Drain again. Trim and cut a cross in the root end of each onion, then slip off the skins.

After 1 hour, add the onions, tomatoes, carrots, and salt and pepper to taste to the veal. Continue to simmer until the veal is tender, another 30–45 minutes. Discard the herb bouquet. If the broth is thin, stir a little into the cornstarch mixture and stir into the stew until slightly thickened. Add the coarsely chopped sage and a few drops of lemon juice. Simmer for 5 minutes.

Spoon onto warmed plates, garnish with the parsley-sage mixture and serve.

SERVES 4

ROAST FILLET OF BEEF WITH MADEIRA SAUCE

1 center-cut beef fillet, 2 lb (1 kg), trimmed of any fat, with a thin
   piece of pork backfat tied on top in several places *(see notes)*
Unsalted butter
Salt and freshly ground pepper
⅓ cup (2 oz/60 g) finely chopped shallots (about 5 shallots)
¼ cup (2 fl oz/60 ml) water
½ cup (4 fl oz/125 ml) Madeira wine
1 teaspoon cornstarch mixed with 1 tablespoon water
¾ cup (6 fl oz/180 ml) heavy (double) cream
Chopped fresh parsley

Position a rack in the bottom third of an oven and preheat to 425°F (220°C).
※ Butter the ends and bottom of the beef fillet and place in a small, heavy roast-ing pan (without a rack) in which it fits comfortably. Sprinkle the meat with salt and pepper. Place in the oven and roast until an instant-read thermometer inserted in the center of the meat registers 120°F (49°C) for rare or 130°F (54°C) for medium-rare, 20–30 minutes. Transfer to a warmed serving plate and cover loosely with a piece of aluminum foil to keep it warm. It will continue to cook a little.
※ Using a large spoon, skim off the fat from the pan juices. Place the pan over medium-low heat and add the shallots. Cook, stirring, until translucent, 3–4 minutes. Add the water, raise the heat to medium and stir, scraping up any browned bits stuck to the pan bottom. Add the Madeira, bring to a boil over medium heat and boil until reduced by about one-half. Combine the cornstarch mixture and the cream and stir until blended. Add to the pan and quickly stir into the juices. Cook, stirring, until slightly thickened, 1–2 minutes. Season to taste with salt and pepper.
※ Cut the strings on the fillet, then remove the strip of fat tied to the top of the fillet and discard. Using a very sharp, thin-bladed knife, slice the meat crosswise into 12–14 slices, each about ½ inch (12 mm) thick. Spoon a little of the sauce onto each warmed plate and place 2 or 3 slices of meat on the sauce. Spoon the remaining sauce over the meat, garnish with the chopped parsley and serve.

SERVES 4

NOTES

As this recipe illustrates, the French are expert at roasting good-quality cuts of beef. The center cut of the fillet (sometimes called the tender-loin) is the best choice here, as its even thickness ensures uniform roasting. The fillet should be well trimmed of any fat. Because the fillet has no internal layer of fat, it needs a strip of pork backfat tied to it so the meat loses none of its moisture during roasting. Ask your butcher to do this for you.

Before you put the roast in the oven, make sure it is at room tem-perature; to do so, remove it from the refrigerator 30–40 minutes in advance.

I'm surprised by how seldom people think to cook such a homey, uncomplicated dish as this one. The preparation is truly simple, and all you need is some time for the cooking to make sure the lamb shanks become absolutely tender.

If you haven't tried Yukon Gold potatoes before, seek them out for the mashed potatoes. They have a lovely color, a rich flavor and a wonderfully smooth consistency when mashed.

LAMB SHANKS WITH POTATOES

1 bunch small leeks, trimmed and cleaned *(see glossary, page 125)*
4 whole lamb shanks, 3–3½ lb (1.5–1.75 kg) total weight
3 tablespoons olive oil
4 or 5 cloves garlic, sliced
2 teaspoons chopped fresh rosemary, plus rosemary sprigs for garnish
Salt and freshly ground pepper
¾ cup (6 fl oz/180 ml) dry white wine
1½–2 lb (750 g–1 kg) Yukon Gold or other white potatoes, peeled and
   cut lengthwise into quarters
¼ cup (2 fl oz/60 ml) heavy (double) cream, or as needed

Slice the leeks crosswise ½ inch (12 mm) thick. Set aside.

Trim the lamb of any fat and wipe with damp paper towels. In a large, deep frying pan over medium-high heat, warm the oil. When hot but not smoking, add the shanks and brown on all sides, 10–12 minutes. Transfer to a plate.

Reduce the heat to medium-low, add the garlic and sauté for 30–40 seconds. Add the leeks and sauté until translucent, 6–8 minutes.

Return the shanks to the pan, scatter the chopped rosemary over them and sprinkle with salt and pepper. Add the wine, raise the heat to medium-high and bring to a simmer. Reduce the heat to low, cover and simmer until the shanks are very tender when pierced with a knife, 2–2½ hours, turning once or twice during the cooking and adding water to the pan to maintain the original level of liquid.

About 30 minutes before the shanks are ready, place the potatoes in a saucepan with water to cover by 2 inches (5 cm). Add 2 teaspoons salt and bring to a boil over medium heat. Boil, uncovered, until the potatoes are tender when pierced with a sharp knife, 25–30 minutes. Drain, reserving the cooking water. Pass the potatoes through a potato ricer or food mill held over the saucepan. Alternatively, mash them with a potato masher in the pan until free of lumps. Place the pan over medium-low heat and, using a wooden spoon, vigorously beat in ¼–½ cup (2–4 fl oz/60–120 ml) of the cooking water, a little at a time, until the potatoes are smooth and of a good consistency. Then beat in the ¼ cup (2 fl oz/60 ml) cream and salt and pepper to taste until well blended. For a thinner consistency, beat in more cream. Cover to keep warm.

When the lamb shanks are tender, season the sauce with salt and pepper if necessary. Spoon the potatoes onto 4 warmed plates. Place a shank on each plate and spoon the leeks and juices over them. Garnish with rosemary sprigs and serve.

SERVES 4

Food-loving American travelers to Paris raved about this dish during the 1950s and 1960s, a time when anyone with just a few extra dollars could enjoy the pleasures of going to Paris and eating in the best restaurants. I was fortunate to be among those well-fed visitors, and I have long enjoyed re-creating the great combination of flavors in this easy and satisfying recipe.

You can ask your butcher to tie the loin, or you can do it yourself: Trim off all but a thin layer of fat from the loin and tie the loin in 3 or 4 places with kitchen string to hold its shape.

Be careful to hold the pan of Cognac away from the heat when lighting it.

Pork Loin with Orange

1 tablespoon vegetable oil
1 boneless pork loin, 2–2½ lb (1–1.25 kg), tied *(see notes)*
1 white sweet onion, chopped (¾–1 cup/4–5 oz/125–155 g)
5 or 6 carrots, 12–14 oz (375–440 g), peeled and cut crosswise
   into slices ¼ inch (6 mm) thick
¼ cup (2 fl oz/60 ml) Cognac, warmed in a small pan
1 bay leaf
2 fresh thyme sprigs
½ cup (4 fl oz/125 ml) dry white wine
Salt and freshly ground pepper
3 oranges
1½–2 teaspoons Dijon-style mustard
1 teaspoon cornstarch mixed with 2 tablespoons water
Chopped fresh parsley

Position a rack in the lower third of an oven and preheat to 350°F (180°C).

In an ovenproof pot over medium-high heat, warm the oil. Add the meat, fat side down, and brown on all sides, 8–10 minutes. Transfer to a plate. Add the onion, reduce the heat to medium-low and sauté until translucent, 6–7 minutes. Add the carrots, sauté for 1–2 minutes and remove from the heat. Return the pork to the pot, fat side up. Light the Cognac, pour it flaming over the pork and let it burn out.

Tuck the bay leaf and thyme under the loin, add the wine and sprinkle with salt and pepper. Cover and bake until the meat is just tender, 50–60 minutes. Insert an instant-read thermometer into the center; it should read 160°F (71°C).

Meanwhile, shred the zest from 1 of the oranges (see glossary, page 126). Place in a small pan, add water to cover and bring to a boil. Boil for 2–3 minutes, then drain. Squeeze the juice from the same orange plus 1 additional orange. You should have 1 cup (8 fl oz/250 ml). Slice the remaining orange crosswise, then cut each slice in half. Set aside.

Transfer the pork to a warmed platter. Cover loosely with aluminum foil. Skim off the fat from the pot juices. Stir in the mustard, orange juice and zest. Bring to a boil and boil until reduced by half, then reduce the heat to medium-low. Stir a little of the juices into the cornstarch mixture, then stir into the pot juices. Stir until slightly thickened, 2–3 minutes. Season with salt and pepper.

Spoon a little sauce with vegetables onto each warmed plate. Slice the pork and arrange on top of the vegetables. Garnish with the reserved orange slices and parsley and serve at once.

Serves 4

SAUSAGE WITH SAUTÉED CABBAGE

1 head green cabbage, about 2 lb (1 kg), damaged leaves removed
1 slice smoked ham, about 1 lb (500 g) and ¼ inch (6 mm) thick
¼ lb (125 kg) thickly sliced lean smoked bacon, cut into pieces
  ½ inch (12 mm) wide
1 yellow onion, diced (1 cup/4 oz/125 g)
1 tablespoon minced garlic (2 or 3 cloves)
2 carrots, peeled and thinly sliced
8–10 juniper berries, crushed with the flat side of a knife blade
1 bay leaf
½ cup (4 fl oz/125 ml) chicken broth
2 teaspoons white wine vinegar
Salt and freshly ground pepper
1 tablespoon olive oil or vegetable oil
4–6 well-seasoned fresh pork, chicken or veal sausages, 1–1½ lb (500–750 g)
½ cup (3 oz/90 g) seedless sweet red grapes

Using a sharp knife, cut the cabbage in half through the core. Slice each half into ½-inch (12-mm) wedges. Set aside.

🧅 Trim the ham slice of any fat and cut into 4 pieces. Place in a frying pan and add water to cover, bring to a boil over medium-high heat and cook for 1 minute. Remove from the heat and set aside to reduce the saltiness of the ham, 10–15 minutes. Drain, pat dry with paper towels and set aside.

🧅 In a large sauté pan or deep frying pan over medium heat, sauté the bacon, stirring, until golden, beginning to crisp and the fat has been rendered, 3–4 minutes. Drain off most of the fat and discard, leaving the bacon in the pan.

🧅 Return the pan to medium-low heat and add the onion and garlic. Sauté, stirring, until the onion is translucent, 6–7 minutes. Add the carrots, juniper berries and bay leaf and sauté until the carrots begin to soften, 4–5 minutes. Add the broth, vinegar and cabbage. Season to taste with salt and pepper, cover and simmer until the cabbage is tender, 15–20 minutes; turn the cabbage and carrots once or twice during cooking. Taste and adjust the seasonings.

🧅 Meanwhile, in another frying pan over medium heat, warm the oil. When hot but not smoking, add the sausages, cover and cook, turning once, for 5 minutes. Add the ham, cover partially and continue to cook, turning, for 10 minutes. Add the grapes and cook until the sausages and ham are cooked through and browned, another 10 minutes. Place the cabbage on a warmed platter. Arrange the meats and grapes on top of the cabbage. Serve at once.

SERVES 4

Although this dish resembles France's famous *choucroute garnie,* it is made with fresh cabbage instead of sauerkraut, a variation I have enjoyed there as well.

Go to a good butcher for a slice of ham cut from a properly smoked whole ham, which is usually only partially cooked. Seek out some of the excellent fresh sausages that are being made by creative food entrepreneurs and sold in specialty-food shops and some large food markets.

I find that green beans cook better if they are first put into ice water to crisp, and then cooked as quickly as possible. Spreading the beans out in rapidly boiling water helps cook them faster.

If you like mint, try mixing 1 tablespoon of the chopped fresh herb with the beans just before serving. It's a delicious way to enjoy them.

GREEN BEANS WITH SHALLOTS

1 lb (500 g) young, tender green beans, preferably a uniform
    4–5 inches (10–13 cm) long
Ice water to cover
Salt
1 tablespoon unsalted butter
2 oz (60 g) shallots (3 or 4 shallots), thinly sliced crosswise
½ lemon, plus 4 lemon wedges for garnish
Freshly ground pepper
4 fresh mint sprigs

Trim the green beans, discarding any old or large ones, and put them in a shallow dish or pan in which they lie flat. Add ice water to cover and set aside to crisp, 10–15 minutes.

In a sauté pan or deep frying pan in which the beans will lie flat, pour in water to a depth of 2–3 inches (5–7.5 cm). Bring to a boil over high heat. When the water is boiling vigorously, drain the beans and plunge them into the boiling water. Add 2 teaspoons salt. When the water returns to a boil, continue to boil until the beans are just tender but still crisp, 4–5 minutes. Drain and immediately plunge into cold water to stop the cooking; then drain again. Set aside.

Pour off the water from the pan if you have not already done so and place the pan over medium-low heat. Add the butter; when it is melted and foaming, add the shallots. Sauté, stirring, until translucent, 1–2 minutes; do not allow to brown. Add the beans and squeeze on a few drops of the juice from the lemon half. Season to taste with salt and pepper. Toss until the beans are evenly seasoned and hot.

Using tongs, arrange the beans on a warmed serving plate. Spoon the shallots over the beans. Garnish the plate with the lemon wedges and mint sprigs and serve at once.

SERVES 4

BAKED BEETS WITH ONION AND CREAM

6 medium-sized beets, about 3 lb (1.5 kg) total weight
2 tablespoons unsalted butter
1 white sweet onion, cut into small dice
2–3 tablespoons water
1 cup (8 fl oz/250 ml) heavy (double) cream
Salt and freshly ground pepper
Chopped fresh parsley

Position a rack in the middle of an oven and preheat to 450°F (230°C).

Cut off the tops of the beets, leaving about ½ inch (12 mm) of stem intact. Do not cut off the root ends or peel or otherwise cut into the beets. Rinse well and pat dry with paper towels. Place the beets on a large piece of aluminum foil, bring the foil up around the beets to enclose fully and fold over the top to seal. Using a knife, make a small slit in the top of the packet for steam to escape and place in a baking pan, folded side up.

Bake until the beets are tender when pierced with the tip of a sharp, thin-bladed knife, 50–60 minutes or more, depending upon the size and age of the beets. Test for doneness after about 45 minutes of baking. Remove from the oven and open the package partway to let the beets cool a little. Reduce the oven temperature to 375°F (190°C).

When cool enough to handle, cut off the stem and root end from each beet. Using your fingers, or with the aid of a paring knife, peel off the skins; they should slip off easily. Cut the beets crosswise into slices about ⅛ inch (3 mm) thick and arrange, layered in straight rows or in concentric circles, in a baking dish. Set aside.

In a sauté pan or frying pan over medium-low heat, melt the butter. When foaming, add the onion and sauté gently, stirring, until translucent, 6–7 minutes. Add the water, cover and steam over low heat until the onion is tender, 8–10 minutes. Watch carefully so that the onion does not burn or brown. When the moisture has evaporated, add the cream and salt and pepper to taste. Raise the heat to medium, bring the cream to a boil and then cook for 1 minute. Remove from the heat and pour the cream-onion mixture evenly over the beets. Bake, uncovered, until the sauce is bubbly, 10–15 minutes.

Sprinkle with chopped parsley and serve immediately directly from the dish.

SERVES 4

NOTES

The French have always baked their beets, and for good reason: the resulting taste and texture are much more intense and complex than those of boiled beets. Do try them. You will find this an excellent companion to a simple grilled steak or chop.

FLAGEOLET BEANS WITH CREAM

Prepared in this way, flageolets are delicious alongside grilled lamb, chicken or fish. You can also serve them on their own as a warm first course.

Now grown in the United States, dried domestic flageolet beans can be found along with imported varieties in specialty-food shops and the international section of some large food stores. I have found that the domestic beans are smaller and not as old as some of the imported varieties, and thus cook in less time.

1½ cups (10½ oz/330 g) dried flageolet beans
2 fresh thyme sprigs
2 fresh parsley sprigs
1 bay leaf
1 celery stalk, cut crosswise into 4 equal pieces
1 small white sweet onion, stuck with 2 whole cloves
Salt
1 tablespoon sour cream
1½–2 teaspoons Dijon-style mustard
½–¾ cup (4–6 fl oz/125–180 ml) heavy (double) cream
2 teaspoons chopped fresh tarragon, plus more to taste, if needed
Freshly ground pepper

Sort through the beans, discarding any damaged beans or small stones. Rinse and drain. Place in a large saucepan and add water to cover by 2 inches (5 cm). Bring to a boil over high heat, remove from the heat, cover and set aside to soak for 1 hour.

Drain, rinse and return the beans to the saucepan with water to cover by 1 inch (2.5 cm). Place the thyme and parsley sprigs and bay leaf inside the celery pieces and tie securely with kitchen string to form a bouquet garni. Add to the pan along with the clove-studded onion and ½ teaspoon salt. Bring to a boil over medium-high heat, reduce the heat to low, cover partially and simmer gently until the beans are tender, 30–45 minutes; the timing will depend upon the size and age of the beans.

Remove and discard the herb bouquet and the onion. Let cool for 10 minutes, then drain the beans and return them to the pan. In a small bowl, combine the sour cream and mustard to taste and mix well. Add the heavy cream to taste, stir until well blended, and then stir in 1 teaspoon of the tarragon. Add the cream mixture to the beans, stir gently to blend and place over medium-low heat. Warm gently to serving temperature. Season to taste with salt, pepper and more mustard, cream or tarragon if needed. Do not stir too much or the beans will become mushy.

Transfer to a warmed serving dish or spoon onto warmed plates. Sprinkle evenly with the remaining tarragon and serve immediately.

SERVES 4

BROCCOLI GRATIN

2 or 3 slices coarse country French or Italian bread
1 bunch broccoli, about 1¼ lb (625 g)
Salt
2 cups (16 fl oz/500 ml) milk
2 tablespoons unsalted butter
2 tablespoons all-purpose (plain) flour
½ cup (2 oz/60 g) shredded Gruyère cheese
Freshly ground pepper
Freshly grated nutmeg

Position a rack in the top third of an oven and preheat to 200°F (95°C). Remove the crusts from the bread and discard. Tear the bread into small pieces and place in a food processor fitted with the metal blade or in a blender. Pulse to form fine crumbs. You should have 2 cups (4 oz/125 g). Spread the crumbs on a baking sheet and place in the oven to dry out; do not allow to brown. This will take 4–6 minutes, depending upon how moist the bread is. Remove from the oven and set aside to cool. Increase the oven temperature to 375°F (190°C).

Cut the florets from the broccoli stems. Cut the large florets so that they are all the same size. Using a vegetable peeler or paring knife, peel off the tough skin from the larger main stems. If the stems are very large, cut in half or into quarters lengthwise, and then cut crosswise into 1-inch (2.5-cm) pieces.

Fill a large saucepan three-fourths full with water and bring to a boil. Add the broccoli and 2 teaspoons salt and boil, uncovered, until the florets and stems are just tender, 4–5 minutes. Drain immediately and spread out on a plate to cool.

In a small saucepan, heat the milk until small bubbles appear around the edges of the pan. Set aside. In another saucepan over medium heat, melt the butter. Add the flour and, using a whisk, stir until blended with the butter. Cook, stirring, for 1 minute; do not allow to brown. Gradually add the milk, whisking or stirring constantly. Continue whisking or stirring, regularly scraping the bottom and sides of the pan, until thickened, 3–4 minutes. Add ⅛ teaspoon salt and cook gently for another 1–2 minutes. Add the cheese and stir until the cheese melts and is blended. Season to taste with salt, pepper and a little nutmeg. Set aside.

In a 1½-qt (1.5-l) baking dish, arrange the broccoli in a single layer. Spoon the sauce evenly over the broccoli and then scatter the bread crumbs over the top. Bake until the crumbs are golden and the sauce is bubbly, 10–15 minutes. Serve at once directly from the dish.

SERVES 4

NOTES

Gratins are some of France's most appealing dishes, from first course to last. The word translates as "crust," describing the golden, often crisp surface that develops when a relatively thin layer of food is baked with a sauce and topping in a broad, shallow baking dish.

The gratin offered here is an excellent way to serve broccoli. It can be prepared in advance up to the point when it goes into the oven. If you like, add to the baking dish 1½ pounds (750 g) tiny pearl onions, blanched for 3 minutes and peeled.

BAKED EGGPLANT AND TOMATO

This simple side dish is found almost everywhere in the south of France. You might recognize it as a version of the familiar vegetable stew known as ratatouille, of which there are many variations. It is equally good served at room temperature.

If you cannot find fresh thyme and oregano, substitute ¼ teaspoon of each of them dried.

1 eggplant (aubergine), about 1 lb (500 g)
Olive oil for brushing, plus 2 tablespoons olive oil
1 lb (500 g) ripe plum (Roma) tomatoes
1 tablespoon chopped garlic (about 3 cloves)
1 yellow onion, finely diced (about 1 cup/5 oz/155 g)
1 green bell pepper (capsicum), seeded, deribbed and cut lengthwise into
   slices ½ inch (12 mm) wide
½ teaspoon chopped fresh thyme
½ teaspoon chopped fresh oregano
Salt and freshly ground pepper

Preheat a broiler (griller). Cut the eggplant in half lengthwise and place on an oiled baking sheet, cut side down. Brush the skin of each eggplant half with olive oil and, using a fork, pierce the skin in 6 or 7 places. Place under the broiler with the top of the eggplant about 4 inches (10 cm) from the heat source. Broil (grill) until the skin is blistered and beginning to blacken, 15–20 minutes. Remove, cover loosely with aluminum foil and set aside to cool. The eggplant will continue to steam for a few minutes.

♨ Core, peel and seed the tomatoes (see glossary, page 124). Chop coarsely; you should have about 2 cups (12 oz/375 g). Set aside.

♨ When the eggplant halves are cool enough to handle, using your fingers, carefully remove the skin. Cut the eggplant halves crosswise into slices ½ inch (12 mm) thick. Place the slices in an oiled oval or rectangular baking dish in a single layer or layered slightly, depending upon the size of the dish. Set aside.

♨ Position a rack in the upper third of an oven and preheat to 350°F (180°C). In a sauté pan or frying pan over medium-low heat, warm the 2 tablespoons olive oil. When hot but not smoking, add the garlic and sauté, stirring, until it begins to change color, 20–30 seconds. Add the onion and sauté, stirring, until translucent, 6–7 minutes. Add the tomatoes, bell pepper, thyme and oregano, cover partially and cook, stirring occasionally, until the tomatoes have broken down, 10–15 minutes. Season to taste with salt and pepper.

♨ Spoon the tomato mixture evenly over the eggplant, cover loosely with aluminum foil and bake until bubbly, 25–30 minutes. Serve immediately directly from the dish.

SERVES 4

POTATO AND ONION GRATIN

The potatoes, onions and garlic in this crusty gratin require a good deal of baking time for absolute tenderness. Make sure the baking dish you choose is large enough for the top of the potatoes to be well below the rim; otherwise, the milk and cream may bubble over.

The potatoes should be sliced to a uniform thickness so they cook evenly. A mandoline is a good tool for slicing the potatoes.

Any leftovers can be reheated in a 300°F (150°C) oven for 8–10 minutes.

2 teaspoons minced garlic (about 2 cloves)
2 lb (1 kg) baking potatoes (about 4), peeled and thinly cut crosswise into slices of uniform thickness
Salt and freshly ground pepper
Freshly ground nutmeg
1 white sweet onion, peeled, halved lengthwise and each half thinly sliced lengthwise
1 cup (8 fl oz/250 ml) milk
1 cup (8 fl oz/250 ml) heavy (double) cream

Position a rack in the middle of an oven and preheat to 375°F (190°C). Butter a 1½- or 2-qt (1.5- or 2-l) oval or rectangular baking dish.

Sprinkle the garlic over the bottom of the baking dish. Layer half of the potato slices, in overlapping rows, over the garlic. Sprinkle lightly with salt, pepper and nutmeg. Spread the onion slices evenly over the potatoes, then layer the remaining potato slices over the top, arranging them attractively. Carefully pour the milk over the potatoes, moistening all of the potato slices as you do. Then pour ½ cup (4 fl oz/125 ml) of the cream over the potato slices, also being careful to moisten all of the slices. Sprinkle to taste with salt, pepper and nutmeg.

Bake until the potatoes are very tender when pierced with the tip of a knife, golden brown on top and have absorbed most of the milk and cream, 1–1½ hours. During the first 40 minutes of baking, baste the potatoes every 10 minutes by tipping the dish a little and scooping up the liquid with a large spoon. Be sure to baste all of the potato slices so that an even golden coating forms. During the last 20–40 minutes of baking, baste the potatoes every 10 minutes with the remaining ½ cup (4 fl oz/125 ml) cream, again being sure to coat all of the slices. You may not need all of the cream.

Remove from the oven and serve directly from the dish.

SERVES 4

STUFFED ZUCCHINI

6 zucchini (courgettes), 5–6 oz (155–185 g) each and not longer
  than 8 inches (20 cm)
2 tablespoons unsalted butter
¼ cup (¾ oz/20 g) minced green (spring) onion, including tender
  green tops (6 or 7 onions)
½ lb (250 g) smoked ham, trimmed of any fat and minced
1 cup (4 oz/125 g) fine dried bread crumbs *(see page 91)*
Salt and freshly ground pepper

FOR THE TOMATO SAUCE:
1 lb (500 g) ripe plum (Roma) tomatoes
2 tablespoons unsalted butter
1 large clove garlic, minced
¼ cup (1½ oz/45 g) minced yellow onion
½ teaspoon minced fresh oregano or ¼ teaspoon dried oregano
½ small green bell pepper (capsicum), seeded, deribbed and minced

With a filling of bread crumbs and
ham and a fragrant tomato sauce
on top, this pleasing recipe
reminds me of the kind of French
country cooking found in a village
restaurant. Serve it as a side dish
with roast or grilled meats, poultry
or seafood; or offer it on its own
for a light lunch or supper,
accompanied with a green salad.
  Purchase a piece of good-quality
smoked ham from your butcher.

Fill a large saucepan three-fourths full with water and bring to a boil. Add the
zucchini and parboil for 2–3 minutes. Drain, cool and slice in half lengthwise.
Scoop out the pulp from each half, leaving walls ¼ inch (6 mm) thick; reserve
the pulp. Lightly salt the cut sides and invert on a rack to drain for 30 minutes.
Finely chop the pulp and drain in a sieve, pressing with a spoon. Set aside.

Position a rack in the top third of an oven and preheat the oven to 375°F
(190°C). Butter a 9-by-13-inch (23-by-33-cm) rectangular baking dish.

In a sauté pan over medium-low heat, melt the butter. Add the green onion and
sauté until translucent, 1–2 minutes. Add the ham and sauté for 4–5 minutes. Add
the zucchini pulp and sauté until the moisture evaporates, 4–5 minutes. Remove
from the heat and stir in half of the bread crumbs. Season with salt and pepper.

Pat the zucchini halves dry with paper towels and place in the prepared dish cut-
side up. Fill the cavities with the ham mixture, rounding the tops if necessary.
Cover evenly with the remaining bread crumbs and bake until the crumbs are
golden and the zucchini is tender when pierced with a knife tip, 30–40 minutes.

Meanwhile, make the sauce: Core, seed and peel the tomatoes (see glossary,
page 124). Chop coarsely. In a saucepan over medium-low heat, melt the butter.
Add the garlic and yellow onion and sauté until translucent, 3–4 minutes. Add
the tomatoes, oregano and bell pepper, raise the heat to medium and sauté until
the tomatoes are soft, 20–25 minutes. Season with salt and pepper.

Place the zucchini on warmed plates and top with the sauce.

SERVES 4

Not all of the omelets made in France are the traditional fluffy kind folded around a filling. Some, like this one, are more rustic pan-cakelike omelets in which the eggs and filling are combined. I find these *omelettes plates* easier to pre-pare, and equally good. This is a splendid dish to serve at a week-end lunch accompanied by a green salad.

For best results, make sure the pan is very hot before adding the butter. Test by flicking a few drops of water into the pan. The drops should sizzle and dance on the sur-face and immediately evaporate. When you add the soft butter, it should melt right away, spread out and foam.

ARTICHOKE FLAT OMELET

Juice of 1 lemon
Salt
1 lb (500 g) baby artichokes, each about 1½ inches (4 cm) in diameter or less
8 thick slices lean smoked bacon, about ½ lb (250 g) total weight
6 eggs
1 tablespoon chopped fresh tarragon
2 tablespoons milk
Freshly ground pepper
3 tablespoons unsalted butter, at room temperature
2–3 tablespoons heavy (double) cream

Fill a large saucepan three-fourths full with water. Add the lemon juice and 2 teaspoons salt. Working with 1 artichoke at a time, trim off the stem even with the bottom. Starting at the base, remove 3 or 4 layers of leaves until you reach tender, pale green leaves. Using a sharp knife, cut off the top half of the artichoke, then cut lengthwise into quarters and plunge them into the lemon water. When all of the artichokes have been trimmed, place the pan over medium-high heat and bring to a boil. Boil gently, uncovered, until the artichokes are tender, 10–15 minutes. Drain and set aside.

In a large frying pan over medium heat, gently fry the bacon slices until evenly golden and crisp on both sides, about 4 minutes total. Using tongs or a slotted utensil, transfer to paper towels to drain. Set aside and cover to keep warm.

Preheat a broiler (griller). In a bowl, combine the eggs, half of the tarragon, the milk, and salt and pepper to taste. Whisk quickly until blended.

Place a heavy, flameproof 10-inch (25-cm) omelet pan or frying pan, preferably nonstick, over medium heat and heat until hot. When hot, immediately add the butter and allow it to melt, tilting the pan until the bottom is completely coated and the butter foams. Pour in the egg mixture and immediately reduce the heat to medium-low. Cook slowly, shaking the pan occasionally. When the eggs are lightly golden on the bottom, in 2–3 minutes, arrange the quartered artichokes over the surface. Spoon the cream to taste evenly over the surface and place the pan under the broiler about 5 inches (13 cm) from the heat source. Broil (grill) until there is a touch of browning but the eggs are still soft and a little runny, 2–3 minutes. Immediately remove from the broiler.

Using a wide spatula, slide the omelet onto a warmed serving plate. Garnish with the remaining chopped tarragon. Cut into wedges and serve with the bacon.

SERVES 4

CHEESE SOUFFLÉ WITH TOMATO-BASIL SAUCE

Tomato-Basil Sauce *(recipe on page 118)*
1 cup (8 fl oz/250 ml) milk
2 tablespoons unsalted butter
2 tablespoons all-purpose (plain) flour
4 egg yolks, at room temperature
½ cup (2 oz/60 g) shredded Gruyère cheese
½ cup (2 oz/60 g) freshly grated Parmesan cheese
Salt and freshly ground pepper
Cayenne pepper
1 tablespoon Madeira wine
5 egg whites, at room temperature
Pinch of cream of tartar

Make the Tomato-Basil Sauce and set aside. Position a rack in the middle of an oven and preheat to 350°F (180°C).

In a small saucepan, heat the milk until small bubbles appear around the edges of the pan. In another saucepan over medium heat, melt the butter. When foaming, add the flour and, using a whisk, stir until blended. Cook, stirring, for 1 minute; do not allow to brown. Gradually add the milk, whisking constantly. Continue whisking, regularly scraping the bottom and sides of the pan, until the mixture thickens and comes to a boil, 2–3 minutes. Cook for a few seconds more until thickened and smooth, then remove from the heat. Let cool a little.

In a bowl, whisk the egg yolks until pale yellow, 1–2 minutes. Gradually whisk the hot sauce into the yolks, then add the cheeses, salt and pepper to taste, a sprinkling of cayenne and the Madeira. Stir to mix well. Set aside.

Place the egg whites in a large, clean, dry bowl. Add the cream of tartar and, using a clean whisk or beaters, beat until soft peaks form and hold their shape. Spoon about one-fourth of the egg whites into the sauce and, using a rubber spatula, stir gently to blend. Then, gently fold the remaining egg whites into the sauce just until incorporated. Spoon the mixture into an ungreased 1½-qt (1.5-l) soufflé dish and bake until puffed and lightly browned, 35–40 minutes.

Warm the Tomato-Basil Sauce gently over medium-low heat.

Remove the soufflé from the oven and carry it immediately to the table before it begins to fall. Spoon onto warmed plates and top each serving with a spoonful of the sauce. Pass the remaining sauce.

SERVES 4

NOTES

It is often said in France that guests must wait for a soufflé; a soufflé will never wait for them. You must, indeed, serve it immediately so that it may be appreciated in all its well-risen glory.

A cheese soufflé is probably the easiest to make of all baked soufflés. Its success will depend upon the sauce being made properly, the egg whites being beaten to the correct degree and the two being folded together but not overmixed.

When you put the soufflé mixture into the prepared dish, the top of the mixture should be about 1 inch (2.5 cm) below the rim. If the mixture is higher than that, you will need to wrap a paper collar around the rim to prevent the soufflé from running over during baking. To make a collar, cut a piece of waxed paper long enough to wrap around the dish. Fold it in half lengthwise and wrap it around the dish with the paper extending 1–2 inches (2.5–5 cm) above the rim. Tie firmly in place with kitchen string.

Pear Tart with Walnuts

I especially like this style of French tart, in which a shallow layer of fruit tops thinly rolled pastry. For best results in pastry making, be sure the dough is pliable and not sticky when you gather it into a ball. If it is too soft and sticky, knead on a floured board a couple of times.

I use Comice pears in the recipe, but the firmer Bosc variety is also excellent. You may find, however, that you will have to poach the Bosc pears a little longer or bake the tart for a few more minutes than what is indicated here.

The tart makes a perfect end to a small dinner party. Any leftovers are delightful the next day with coffee.

1 cup (5 oz/155 g) all-purpose (plain) flour
½ cup (2 oz/60 g) cake (soft-wheat) flour
1 tablespoon plus 1½ cups (12 oz/375 g) sugar
¼ teaspoon salt
½ cup (4 oz/125 g) unsalted butter, chilled, cut into small cubes
2–3 tablespoons ice water
3 cups (24 fl oz/750 ml) cold water, or as needed
3 ripe but firm pears such as Comice or Bosc, peeled, halved,
   cored and tossed in a bowl with the juice of 1 lemon
½ cup (5 oz/155 g) apricot preserves, forced through a sieve
1 cup (4 oz/125 g) walnut pieces
Whipped cream topping *(recipe on page 110 or 112)*

Position a rack in the lower third of an oven and preheat to 400°F (200°C).

In a bowl, mix together the flours, the 1 tablespoon sugar and the salt. Using a pastry blender or your fingertips, cut the butter into the flour mixture until it resembles oatmeal. Tossing the mixture with a fork, slowly add the ice water just until the mixture holds together. Gather into a ball, flatten into a round and place between 2 pieces of plastic wrap. Roll out into a round 12 inches (30 cm) in diameter. Peel off the top sheet of plastic wrap. Invert the dough round over a 9-inch (23-cm) fluted tart pan with a removable bottom. Peel off the other piece of plastic wrap and fit the dough into the pan. Cut off the excess even with the rim. Chill.

In a deep frying pan over medium heat, combine the cold water and the 1½ cups (12 oz/375 g) sugar. Bring to a boil and stir to dissolve the sugar. Add the pears and lemon juice and bring back to a simmer; add water as needed just to cover the pears. Reduce the heat to medium-low and simmer, turning once, until almost tender, about 15 minutes. Transfer the pears to a rack placed over a baking pan. Let cool.

Spread most of the preserves over the bottom of the tart shell. Cut each pear half crosswise into thin slices, keeping them together. Transfer the pears to the shell with the stem ends facing the center. Brush with the remaining preserves. Fill the spaces between them with the walnuts.

Bake until the crust is golden, 1–1¼ hours. Let cool on a rack, then remove the outer ring and slide the tart onto a flat plate. Serve warm or at room temperature with the whipped cream.

SERVES 4

CHOCOLATE MOUSSE

Candied Orange Peel *(recipe on page 118)*
½ teaspoon instant espresso powder
1 tablespoon boiling water
⅛ teaspoon ground cardamom
4 oz (125 g) bittersweet chocolate, preferably a dark, rich
    chocolate, broken or chopped into small pieces
2 tablespoons unsalted butter
4 eggs, separated
1 tablespoon sugar
⅛ teaspoon cream of tartar
4 fresh mint sprigs

Make the Candied Orange Peel ahead of time.

In a cup, dissolve the espresso powder in the boiling water, stir in the ground cardamom and set aside.

Place the chocolate and butter in a heatproof bowl and set over (but not touching) 1 inch (2.5 cm) of barely simmering water in a saucepan. Let melt, stirring occasionally. When melted, add the espresso mixture and stir until blended and smooth. Remove from the heat.

In a separate bowl, combine the egg yolks and the 1 tablespoon sugar and, using a whisk, beat until increased in volume and very light, 3–4 minutes. While stirring the melted chocolate with a wooden spoon or rubber spatula, gradually add the beaten yolks, then beat until the chocolate is thickened.

Place the egg whites and cream of tartar in another clean, dry bowl. Using a clean whisk or beaters, beat until stiff peaks form that hold their shape but are not dry. Add about one-fourth of the beaten whites to the chocolate mixture and, using a rubber spatula, stir gently to blend. Then add the remaining egg whites and gently fold in just until incorporated. Pour into a serving bowl. Cover the bowl with paper towels (this absorbs any condensation that forms); make sure the towels do not touch the mousse. Refrigerate for several hours until well set.

At the table, spoon the mousse into shallow dessert bowls or deep dessert plates. Place several strips of Candied Orange Peel alongside each serving. Pass the rest in a bowl at the table. Garnish each serving with a mint sprig.

SERVES 4

NOTES

If you have never eaten chocolate mousse as it is served in a good French bistro or restaurant, you've missed out on an outstanding dessert. The traditional mousse is exceptionally light and very simple. I have added a little espresso powder and cardamom here, which gives the mousse a marvelous new dimension of flavor.

When making the mousse, take care not to overbeat the egg whites or they will become dry and start to break apart. Whites beaten with a light hand will mix most successfully into the chocolate, without losing much of their loft.

In France, this mousse is usually served at the table from a large glass or porcelain bowl. You can, however, spoon it into individual dishes. The candied orange peel adds considerably to this dessert, plus it is delicious eaten with after-dinner coffee.

WALNUT WAFERS

Thin nut wafers are a perfect accompaniment to fruit desserts. One easy-to-make batch yields an abundance.

The cookies should crisp up right after baking. Let the first batch cool for a few minutes, then check to see if they are crisp. If not, bake the second batch a little longer.

Being crisp sugar cookies, they attract moisture, so store them in airtight containers to keep them fresh and brittle. They will keep for up to 3 or 4 days in a cool, dry place.

2 tablespoons all-purpose (plain) flour
½ teaspoon salt
½ teaspoon baking soda (bicarbonate of soda)
½ cup (4 oz/125 g) unsalted butter, at room temperature
1 cup (8 oz/250 g) sugar
2 eggs
1 teaspoon vanilla extract (essence)
1½ cups (6 oz/185 g) chopped walnuts

Position a rack in the middle of an oven and a second one in the upper part; preheat to 375°F (190°C). Line 2 or more baking sheets with parchment paper or waxed paper and set aside.

In a bowl, sift together the flour, salt and baking soda and set aside.

In another bowl, combine the butter and sugar and, using an electric mixer set on medium speed, beat until light and creamy, 5–6 minutes, scraping the sides of the bowl occasionally with a rubber spatula. Add 1 of the eggs and continue to beat at medium speed until fully incorporated. Add the remaining egg and again beat in thoroughly. Beat in the vanilla extract. Using a rubber spatula, fold in the flour mixture and then the walnuts.

Using a teaspoon, place spoonfuls of the batter about 3 inches (7.5 cm) apart on the prepared baking sheets; the wafers will need space to spread. Bake until brown around the edges, 8–10 minutes. Using a thin spatula, immediately remove the wafers from the paper and place on a wire rack to cool. They should be very crisp. Store in an airtight container.

MAKES 80–85 COOKIES

CHERRY CLAFOUTI

1 lb (500 g) fresh dark sweet cherries, such as Bing or Lambert
1 cup (8 fl oz/250 ml) milk
¼ cup (2 fl oz/60 ml) heavy (double) cream
½ cup (1½ oz/45 g) sifted cake (soft-wheat) flour
4 eggs, at room temperature
½ cup (4 oz/125 g) granulated sugar
⅛ teaspoon salt
1 tablespoon kirsch or 1 teaspoon pure almond extract (essence)
Confectioners' (icing) sugar for dusting
Fresh mint leaves

Position a rack in the upper third of an oven and preheat to 350°F (180°C).
Butter a 1½-qt (1.5-l) round, oval or rectangular baking dish with low sides. A
10-inch (25-cm) round pie dish with sides 2 inches (5 cm) deep is a good choice.
🌸 Using a cherry pitter, pit the cherries. Arrange the cherries in the prepared
baking dish in a single layer. They should just cover the bottom of the dish.
Set aside.
🌸 In a saucepan over medium-low heat, combine the milk and cream and heat
until small bubbles appear along the edges of the pan; do not boil. Remove from
the heat and, using a whisk, vigorously whisk in the flour, a little at a time, until
well blended and no lumps remain. Set aside.
🌸 In a bowl, combine the eggs, granulated sugar and salt and, using the whisk,
beat until light and creamy. Add the milk mixture and the kirsch or almond
extract and whisk until well blended and smooth.
🌸 Pour over the cherries; it should just cover them. Place the baking dish on a
baking sheet and place in the oven. Bake until browned and puffed yet still soft
in the center and a sharp, thin-bladed knife stuck into the center of the custard
comes out almost clean, 45–55 minutes. Transfer to a rack to cool slightly.
🌸 Dust the top generously with confectioners' sugar. Using a large serving spoon,
place 2 or 3 spoonfuls on each dessert plate. Dust with more confectioners' sugar
and garnish with mint leaves. Serve warm.

SERVES 4

Clafouti, a traditional specialty
from the Limousin district of
France, is dessert making at its
simplest. All you need to ensure
success are ripe, dark sweet
cherries. It is also best to remove
their pits with a cherry pitter;
cutting them open with a knife
results in too much juice being
released into the batter.

To measure sifted flour, spoon
the flour into a sifter while holding
the sifter over the appropriately
sized measuring cup. Then sift until
the cup is full. Use a straight-edged
knife to level off the flour even
with the rim.

BITTERSWEET CHOCOLATE CAKE

True chocolate purists will love this cake. It has a fine flavor without being too rich, and it does not need an icing.

A springform pan is the best choice, but a pan with a solid bottom may also be used. If you settle on the latter, be sure to butter the pan well, cut a piece of waxed paper to fit the bottom precisely, slip it into the pan, butter the paper and then dust the paper well with flour.

The cake tastes best served warm. Reheat any leftovers in a 200°F (93°C) oven for 4–5 minutes.

3 tablespoons cake (soft-wheat) flour
1 tablespoon unsweetened cocoa
2 teaspoons instant espresso powder
5 oz (155 g) bittersweet chocolate, chopped into chunks
6 tablespoons (3 oz/90 g) unsalted butter, cut into small cubes, at room temperature
4 eggs, separated
½ cup (3½ oz/105 g) superfine (castor) sugar
1 teaspoon pure vanilla extract (essence)

FOR THE WHIPPED CREAM TOPPING:
1 cup (8 fl oz/250 ml) heavy (double) cream
2 tablespoons sour cream
2 tablespoons confectioners' (icing) sugar
1 tablespoon finely grated orange zest (see glossary, page 126)
1 teaspoon pure vanilla extract (essence)

Confectioners' (icing) sugar for dusting

Position a rack in the middle of an oven and preheat to 350°F (180°C). Butter and flour an 8-inch (20-cm) springform pan with 2-inch (5-cm) sides.

In a bowl, sift together the flour, cocoa and espresso powder. Set aside.

Place the chocolate in a heatproof bowl and set over (but not touching) barely simmering water in a saucepan. Melt, stirring occasionally, then remove from the heat and stir in the butter, a little at a time, until blended. Let cool slightly.

In a large bowl, combine the egg yolks and superfine sugar. Using an electric mixer set on medium speed, beat until creamy, 3–4 minutes. Beat in the chocolate mixture until blended. Fold in the flour mixture and then the vanilla.

Beat the egg whites until soft peaks form. Stir one-fourth of the whites into the batter. Fold in the remaining whites just until incorporated.

Pour into the prepared pan and level the top. Bake until the top is risen and crusty and a toothpick stuck into the center comes out almost clean, 30–35 minutes. The center should be soft and moist. Let cool on a wire rack for 10–15 minutes. The top will fall a bit. Remove the pan sides. Loosen the cake's edges with a knife and slide the warm cake onto a serving plate.

In a bowl, whisk together the cream and sour cream until slightly thickened. Beat in the sugar, zest and vanilla until soft folds form. Dust the warm cake with confectioners' sugar. Cut into slices and top with the whipped cream.

MAKES ONE 8-INCH (20-CM) CAKE; SERVES 6–8

Sautéed Apples with Whipped Cream

1 lemon
6 sweet eating apples such as Fuji, Gala or Golden Delicious
  2½–3 lb (1.25–1.5 kg) total weight
6 tablespoons (3 oz/90 g) unsalted butter
1 piece vanilla bean, 2 inches (5 cm) long
¼ cup (2 oz/60 g) granulated sugar

FOR THE WHIPPED CREAM TOPPING:
1 cup (8 fl oz/250 ml) heavy (double) cream
2 tablespoons sour cream
1 tablespoon confectioners' (icing) sugar
1 teaspoon pure vanilla extract (essence)

¼ cup (2 fl oz/60 ml) Calvados or other apple brandy
4 fresh mint sprigs

Squeeze the juice from the lemon into a large bowl. One at a time, peel, quarter and core the apples; then, to keep them from turning dark, immediately place in the bowl and turn in the lemon juice until well coated.

In a large sauté pan or frying pan over medium heat, melt the butter. Using a sharp knife, cut a lengthwise slit in the vanilla bean, but do not cut completely through. Open up the pod and add it to the pan, together with half of the apples. Sauté gently, turning the apples from time to time, until golden, 10–15 minutes. Using tongs, transfer the apples to a plate, leaving the vanilla bean and butter in the pan. Sauté the remaining apples in the same manner. Return the first batch of apples to the pan. Spread out the apples in a single layer and sprinkle evenly with the granulated sugar. Cook over medium heat, turning once, until tender when pierced with the tip of a sharp knife, 10–15 minutes longer.

Meanwhile, make the whipped cream topping: In a bowl, combine the cream and sour cream and whisk (or beat with an electric mixer) until the cream starts to thicken. Add the confectioners' sugar and vanilla extract and continue beating until thickened to soft folds. Cover and refrigerate until ready to use.

When the apples are tender, remove from the heat. In a small saucepan, warm the apple brandy. Holding the pan away from the heat, light the brandy, pour it flaming over the apples and let it burn out. Set aside to cool a little. (If allowed to cool completely, reheat in a 200°F/95°C oven for 4–5 minutes.)

Place 6 warm apple quarters on each dessert plate and top with the whipped cream. Garnish each serving with a mint sprig.

SERVES 4

FRESH FRUIT COMPOTE WITH CASSIS

12–16 Walnut Wafers *(recipe on page 106)*
1 cup (4 oz/125 g) raspberries
1 cup (4 oz/125 g) blueberries
2 oranges
3 tablespoons *sirop de cassis (see notes)*
2 large, ripe mangoes
1 large, ripe Comice or Anjou pear
1 lime
4 small fresh mint sprigs

Make the Walnut Wafers ahead of time and set aside.

🍶 Sort through the raspberries and blueberries and discard any old or bruised berries. Rinse and drain well. Set aside.

🍶 Squeeze the juice from the oranges; you should have about 1 cup (8 fl oz/ 250 ml). Place the juice in a small bowl and stir in the *sirop de cassis.* Set aside.

🍶 Peel each mango, then slice off the flesh in one piece from each side of the flat pit. Cut into ¾-inch (2-cm) dice. Place in a serving bowl. Trim the remaining mango flesh from the narrow side of the pits and add to the bowl.

🍶 Peel the pear, cut into quarters and remove the stem and core. Cut each quarter into ¾-inch (2-cm) dice. Add to the diced mango.

🍶 Add the raspberries and blueberries to the diced fruit. Pour the orange juice mixture over the fruit and stir gently to blend well. Cover and place in the refrigerator to chill for 30–40 minutes before serving.

🍶 To serve, spoon the fruit and their juices into chilled glass compotes. Using a zester or fine-holed shredder and holding the lime over each compote of fruit, shred the zest from the lime directly onto the fruit (see glossary, page 126). The released lime oil will spray over the fruit as well. Garnish each serving with a mint sprig. Serve with the Walnut Wafers.

SERVES 4

NOTES

This simple fruit dessert gains distinction from the addition of *sirop de cassis,* a delicious, non-alcoholic black currant syrup made in France and available in specialty-food shops and in the international section of some large food stores. Do not confuse the syrup with the alcoholic cassis liqueur used in bars for drink making. Other natural berry and fruit syrups will work equally well.

Although you'll find similar desserts in many countries, I think the French can take credit for the origin of floating islands. The dessert has always been one of my favorites, and I have regularly sought it out when I've been in France.

If you've never made floating islands before, I think you'll be surprised by how relatively simple the directions are, and pleased by the fact that they can be made hours ahead of serving. Poaching the meringues can be a little tricky, however. Poach only a couple of them at a time to start with, until you get the hang of it; be careful not to cook them too long. This recipe will make more meringues than you need; serve only the best ones.

ORANGE FLOATING ISLANDS

1 orange
2 cups (16 fl oz/500 ml) milk
5 egg yolks
⅓ cup (2½ oz/75 g) sugar
¼ cup (2 fl oz/60 ml) heavy (double) cream

FOR THE MERINGUES:
4 egg whites
⅛ teaspoon cream of tartar
⅓ cup (2½ oz/75 g) sugar
Unsweetened cocoa for sprinkling
Ground cinnamon for sprinkling

Grate the zest from the orange (see glossary, page 126). Measure 1 tablespoon.
In a saucepan over medium heat, warm the milk until small bubbles appear along the edges of the pan. Remove from the heat. In a bowl, combine the egg yolks and sugar. Whisk until light, 1–2 minutes. Whisk in the cream and orange zest. Then gradually whisk in the hot milk until well blended.
Return the mixture to the saucepan and place over medium-low heat. Stirring with a wooden spoon, heat until thickened and the mixture coats the spoon, about 5 minutes. Do not overcook. To test, run a finger across the back of the spoon; it should leave a trail. Immediately transfer to a shallow serving bowl, set aside to cool a little, then cover and chill.
To make the meringues, in a large sauté pan or deep frying pan, pour in water to a depth of 1 inch (2.5 cm) and bring to a bare simmer over medium-low heat. Meanwhile, in a large, clean, dry bowl, combine the egg whites and cream of tartar. Using a balloon whisk, beat until stiff peaks begin to form. While continuing to whisk, gradually add about half of the sugar, a little at a time, until the whites are glossy and stand in peaks. Using a large spoon, fold in the remaining sugar, a little at a time. The meringue should remain glossy and stand in peaks.
Cover a baking pan with paper towels. Using a serving spoon and forming one at a time, scoop up oval mounds of meringue and float them in the simmering water. Poach, turning once, about 45 seconds on each side. Using a slotted spoon, transfer the meringues to the prepared pan to drain. Repeat with the rest of the meringue. Transfer to a plate, cover and chill for up to 2 hours.
To serve, spoon the custard into shallow dessert bowls or deep dessert plates and float 2 or 3 meringues on each custard. Sprinkle each meringue with a little cocoa and cinnamon and serve.

SERVES 4

BASIC RECIPES

Four fundamental recipes referred to throughout this book.

TOMATO-BASIL SAUCE (PISTOU)

2 ripe tomatoes, about ½ lb (250 g) total weight
¼ teaspoon salt
2 cloves garlic
2 cups (2 oz/60 g) tightly packed fresh basil leaves
2 tablespoons extra-virgin olive oil
Freshly ground pepper

Core, peel and seed the tomatoes (see page 124). Cut into small pieces; set aside. In a food processor fitted with the metal blade or in a blender, combine the salt and garlic cloves. Process until coarsely chopped. Add the basil leaves and continue to process to form a coarse purée, scraping down the sides of the bowl. Add the tomatoes and process until a smooth purée forms. Add the olive oil and pepper to taste and continue to process until well blended and smooth. Taste and adjust the seasonings. Use immediately or transfer to a jar and refrigerate for up to 1 day.

MAKES ABOUT 1¼ CUPS (10 FL OZ/310 ML)

BASIL AIOLI

1 small clove garlic, minced
1 egg yolk, at room temperature
1–2 tablespoons fresh lemon juice
Salt
½ cup (4 fl oz/125 ml) olive oil or vegetable oil
3–4 tablespoons heavy (double) cream
4 tablespoons finely chopped fresh basil leaves
Freshly ground black pepper or ground cayenne pepper

Place the minced garlic in a bowl and mash to a smooth pulp. Add the egg yolk, 1 tablespoon of the lemon juice and a pinch of salt. Whisk until well blended. Add a few drops of the oil and whisk vigorously until thickened. Add a few more drops of the oil and whisk again until an emulsion forms. Continuing to whisk, add the oil, a little at a time, beating vigorously after each addition before adding the next. The mixture should be very thick. Gradually add the cream until the sauce has the consistency of thick cream. Stir in the basil until well blended. Press some of the basil against the side of the bowl with the back of the spoon to release its flavor. Add black pepper or cayenne pepper to taste. Taste and adjust the seasonings. Use immediately or transfer to a jar and refrigerate for up to 1 day.

MAKES 1 CUP (8 FL OZ/250 ML)

CANDIED ORANGE PEEL

2 oranges, preferably with thick skin
1 tablespoon sea salt
1 cup (8 oz/250 g) sugar, plus extra for coating
½ cup (4 fl oz/125 ml) water
3 tablespoons light corn syrup

Cut around the circumference of each orange, cutting only through the peel. Make a second cut around each orange at a right angle to the first, from the stem through the blossom end, and again only cutting through the peel. Carefully remove the peel in 4 segments. In a small bowl, combine the 4 peel pieces and the salt and add water just to cover. Stir to dissolve the salt and let stand for about 4 hours. Drain the peel and place in a small saucepan. Add water to cover and bring to a boil over medium-high heat. Reduce the heat to medium-low and simmer, uncovered, for 15 minutes. Drain and repeat the process. Drain again and set aside to cool. Cut the peel into strips ¼ inch (6 mm) wide. In a small saucepan over medium heat, combine the 1 cup (8 oz/250 g) sugar, the water and corn syrup. Heat, stirring, until the mixture comes to a boil and the sugar is dissolved. Add the peel strips, reduce the heat to low and cook slowly until the peel is translucent and the syrup registers 230°F (110°C) on a candy thermometer, 45–60 minutes. Do not allow to caramelize. Transfer the peel to a wire rack to drain, spreading it out so that the strips do not touch. While the strips are still warm, spread sugar on a plate and roll the peels in the sugar until thoroughly coated. Place on a piece of waxed paper to cool completely and to dry. Store in a tightly covered container in a cool place for up to several weeks.

MAKES 1½–2 CUPS (7½–10 OZ/235–315 G)

COUSCOUS

1 cup (8 fl oz/250 ml) water
2 tablespoons unsalted butter
½ teaspoon salt
1 cup (6 oz/185 g) quick-cooking couscous

In a saucepan over medium-high heat, combine the water, butter and salt. Bring to a boil and remove from the heat. Stir in the couscous, cover and let stand for 5 minutes. Fluff up with a fork and serve.

MAKES 3 CUPS (24 FL OZ/750 ML); SERVES 4 OR 5

Suggested Menus

It is a common misconception that the French eat a banquet at every meal: an hors d'oeuvre, followed by soup or an appetizer, a main course with side dishes, and then a salad, cheese and dessert. While that may apply to special occasions, nothing could be further from the truth of daily life in France. A typical French lunch, for instance, may be as simple as a bowl of soup accompanied by a salad and followed by a light dessert. Use the following menus as examples of how to compose a French-style menu, picking and choosing from among the many varied courses represented by the chapters in this book.

Light Lunches or Brunches

Mediterranean Tuna Salad, page 33
Onion Soup, page 27
Cherry Clafouti, page 109

Leeks à la Grecque, page 11
Artichoke Flat Omelet, page 98
Mango and Melon Salad, page 43
Walnut Wafers, page 106, and Coffee

Cheese Soufflé with Tomato-Basil Sauce, page 101
Green Beans with Shallots, page 84
Pear Tart with Walnuts, page 102

Vegetables with Three Sauces, page 15
Country Veal Stew, page 74
Couscous, page 118
Orange Floating Islands, page 116

Dinners or Light Suppers

Celery Root with Mustard Mayonnaise, page 12
Roast Tarragon Chicken, page 44
Potato and Onion Gratin, page 94
Chicory and Goat Cheese Salad, page 30
Bittersweet Chocolate Cake, page 110

Green Lentil Salad, page 9
Pork Loin with Orange, page 80
Broccoli Gratin, page 91
Endive and Mushroom Salad, page 37
Sautéed Apples with Whipped Cream, page 112

Carrot Soup with Coriander, page 19
Halibut with Hollandaise, page 58
Green Beans with Shallots, page 84
Escarole Salad with Bacon, page 40
Chocolate Mousse, page 105

Asparagus with Orange Hollandaise Sauce, page 6
Rack of Lamb with Flageolet Beans, page 72
Fresh Fruit Compote with Cassis, page 115

Serve a French baguette or a rustic country-style loaf from a local bakery with any of the menus listed here.

Kitchen Equipment

A selection of cookware and tools used in the preparation of the recipes in this collection.

COOKWARE & BAKEWARE

Sturdy pots and pans for stove top and oven.

1. Saucepans
Versatile pans in a wide range of sizes, for cooking many foods. Select pans that absorb heat well and transfer it quickly to the food. Classic French copper is shown here; other good choices include heavy anodized aluminum, cast aluminum, stainless steel and enameled steel.

2. Baking Dish
Select heavy-duty glazed porcelain, stoneware, earthenware, glass or copper for oven baking.

3. Gratin Dish
Shallow baking dish that promotes the formation of a golden crust atop gratins.

4. Soufflé Dish
Classic, deep, straight-sided 1½-quart (1.5-l) circular baking dish for the preparation of soufflés.

5. Sauté Pan
For quick searing or browning or for gentle sautéing, stewing or braising, select a well-made heavy metal pan large enough to hold food in a single layer without crowding. Straight sides help retain heat and contain splattering.

6. Frying or Omelet Pan
French-style pan with gently sloping sides that make cooking and rolling classic omelets easier. Select a heavy metal pan that absorbs heat well and transfers it quickly. The 10-inch (25-cm) size shown here may also be used for sautéing.

7. Stew Pot
Deep pot with ovenproof handle, for cooking stews on the stove top or in the oven. Heavy enameled cast iron (shown here) is a good choice, as it holds heat well.

8. Baking Sheet
All-purpose shallow-rimmed metal baking sheet for such tasks as roasting peppers (capsicums) or eggplants (aubergines), toasting nuts or bread crumbs, or baking cookies and wafers.

9. Baking or Roasting Pan
Heavy, durable metal pan large enough to hold roasts. Sturdy metal V-shaped rack facilitates lifting and turning, promotes even cooking and prevents sticking.

10. Springform Pan
Circular pan with high spring-clip sides that loosen for easy unmolding of delicate cakes.

11. Tart Pan
Shallow baking pan with fluted sides and removable bottom, for attractive shaping and easy unmolding of tarts.

PREP TOOLS

To help speed along food preparation.

12. Food Mill
Hand-cranked mill purées vegetables, soups and fruits by forcing ingredients through its conical grinding disks, which also sieve out fibers, skins and seeds.

13. Ricer
Sturdy, hinged stainless-steel apparatus forces boiled vegetables through small holes, producing smooth, fine-textured mashed potatoes and other purées.

14. Kitchen String
For trussing poultry and tying pork loin and for making bouquets garnis. Select linen string that will withstand intense heat with minimal charring.

15. Cutting Board
Choose a hardwood or good-quality acrylic cutting board for preparing vegetables and meats. Clean thoroughly after every use.

UTENSILS

Hand-held tools for general and specific tasks.

16. Cherry Pitter
Small, sturdy device grips a cherry and pushes out its pit in one squeeze. Can also be used to pit olives.

17. Melon Baller
Small, sharp-edged hemispherical scoop cuts melon or other soft fruits or vegetables into perfectly shaped balls. Can also be used for removing seeds from cucumbers.

18. Zester
Small, sharp holes at end of stainless-steel blade cut citrus zest into fine shreds.

19. Carving Knife
Long serrated blade for cutting bread and roasted meat.

20. Hand-Held Grater
Fine rasp surface for grating cheeses, citrus zest and other ingredients into fine particles.

21. Fine-Holed Shredder
Hand-held utensil perforated with sharp slots for cutting thin shreds of citrus zest or other ingredients.

22. Pastry Blender
Sturdy curved wires for cutting butter or shortening into flour when making pastry by hand.

23. Dry Measuring Cups
In graduated sizes, for measuring dry ingredients. Straight rims allow ingredients to be leveled for accuracy. Choose stainless steel for precision.

24. Measuring Spoons
For measuring small quantities of ingredients such as chopped herbs, salt or baking powder. Select good-quality, calibrated metal spoons with deep bowls.

25. Liquid Measuring Cup & Instant-Read Thermometer
For measuring liquid ingredients, choose a heavy-duty heat-resistant glass cup. Instant-read thermometer provides quick, accurate way to test roasted meat or poultry for doneness.

26. Assorted Utensils
Wide fine-mesh skimmer for removing froth from simmered recipes and for retrieving small pieces of food from simmering liquid; wooden spoons for all-purpose mixing and stirring; stainless-steel wire whisk for beating eggs or blending liquids; long-handled metal tongs for picking up or turning ingredients; slotted spoon for transferring cooked meats or vegetables without their liquid; rubber spatula for gentle blending and folding of batters and soufflé mixtures; and ladle for serving soups and stews.

FRENCH INGREDIENTS

An illustrated primer of distinctive ingredients used in French cooking, all sold in specialty-food stores and well-stocked markets.

BELGIAN ENDIVE

Also known as chicory or witloof, this leaf vegetable has refreshing, slightly bitter, spear-shaped leaves, white to pale yellow-green—or sometimes red—in color, tightly packed in cylindrical heads 4–6 inches (10–15 cm) long. Grown in northern France and Belgium, Belgian endive was developed relatively recently, in the late 19th century, cultivated from the roots of wild chicory.

CALVADOS

Distilled from cider and aged for at least one year in oak casks, this dry, fragrant apple brandy is named for the area of Normandy in which it has been produced for centuries. Sipped on its own as a digestive after dinner, Calvados is also used to flavor both savory and sweet dishes of the region, and is frequently combined with apples.

CHEESES

With hundreds of cheeses produced throughout France, and many dozens exported as well, lovers of French cheese have a wide variety from which to choose. Among these, some of the most popular are goat's milk cheeses (below right), known by the collective French term *chèvre,* which are generally fresh and creamy, with a distinctive tang; they are usually sold shaped into small rounds, and are sometimes coated with pepper, ash or mixtures of herbs, which add mild flavor. Excellent fresh goat cheeses are also now produced in the United States. Also finding favor, particularly as a melted topping for French onion soup and for vegetable gratins, is Gruyère, a variety of Swiss cheese with a firm, smooth texture, small holes and a strong, tangy flavor. Rich, creamy, ripened Brie cheese (below left) is always a French favorite. It is usually sold in wedges cut from whole wheels, with a white, powdery rind.

CHICORY

Grown around Paris and in western France, this curly-leafed salad green—also occasionally cooked as a side dish—is prized for its refreshing bitterness, present most mildly in the pale green to white leaves found at the center of its loose, open head. Also known as curly endive.

COUSCOUS

A North African staple, these small, granular particles of semolina pasta became a French favorite after Algeria was colonized by France in the 1820s. Couscous has a fluffy consistency resembling rice pilaf when cooked, making it an ideal accompaniment to stews, braises or other foods with sauces. Traditional couscous takes as long as 1½ hours to steam. Quick-cooking couscous, available in well-stocked food stores, has been precooked and then redried, and is ready to serve in a matter of minutes.

CRÈME FRAÎCHE

Fresh pasteurized cream is lightly soured and thickened by the addition of lactic bacteria culture to produce this popular product, used throughout France as a topping or enrichment for a wide range of savory and sweet dishes. It may be found in the refrigerated case of well-stocked food markets. To make your own crème fraîche at home, stir  1 teaspoon cultured buttermilk into 1 cup (8 fl oz/250 ml) heavy (double) cream. Cover tightly and leave at warm room temperature until thickened, about 12 hours. Refrigerate until ready to serve. Store for up to 1 week.

DIJON MUSTARD

Among the many varieties of mustard made in France, that produced in and around the leading mustard-producing city of Dijon is distinguished by a pale yellow color and fairly hot, sharp flavor resulting from its blend of brown mustard seeds—or, if marked *blanc,* lighter seeds—and white wine or wine vinegar. Similar non-French blends may be labeled Dijon style.

ESCAROLE

Popular in France both raw in salads and cooked, this variety of chicory has broad, curly, bright green leaves with a refreshingly bitter flavor. Also known as Batavian endive.

FLAGEOLET BEANS

Small and pale green, these popular dried beans, harvested before they reach maturity, come from Brittany in northern France. They are now being grown in the United States as well. Their earthy flavor complements lamb dishes particularly well.

FRENCH BREAD

A wide variety of different breads are produced in France. But the daily bread most often is the *baguette,* a long, slender loaf with a tender, dense white crumb and a well-developed, crisp crust. When "crusty French bread" is suggested as an ingredient or accompaniment to a recipe in this book, widely available French-style baguettes serve the purpose well.

GREEN LENTILS

This popular variety of the small, disk-shaped dried legume may be used in soups, salads or as a side dish. Although lentils originated in Asia, they are grown throughout France today, with the green Puy lentil (from Le Puy in the Auvergne) widely favored and exported.

When preparing any lentils, make sure to pick through them carefully before cooking to remove such impurities as stones, fibers or misshapen beans.

LEEKS

Leeks, which originated in the Middle East, were introduced to France under the Roman Empire. Grown year-round in the northern and western parts of the country, they flavor soups, stews and braises, as well as being enjoyed cooked on their own as appetizers or side dishes. Grown in sandy soil, leeks require thorough cleaning before use (see page 125).

MADEIRA WINE

Ranging from dry to sweet, this amber dessert wine comes from the Portuguese island of Madeira. The labels of most Madeiras include an indication of the type of grapes from which they were made, with Bual and Malmsey being sweetest and fullest in body; Verdelho having a nuttier, more mellow quality; and Sercial being the driest. Madeira wine is popularly drunk as an aperitif in France and is used in sauces and other preparations.

MESCLUN

A specialty of southern France, with a name derived from the Niçois word for "mixture," this assortment of tiny greens is frequently served as a salad on its own or as a garnish or base for other ingredients. Although ingredients will vary, mesclun typically includes chicory (curly endive), lamb's

lettuce and dandelion leaves, combined with such other greens as oak leaf lettuce, chervil, arugula (rocket) and purslane. Well-stocked food stores and greengrocers sometimes carry mesclun, which is often prewashed and bagged for sale.

NIÇOISE OLIVES

Picked when ripe and then pickled in brine, these small, brown to black olives are a specialty of the Provençal city of Nice.

SHALLOTS

Grown in France for well more than a thousand years, these small cousins of the onion have brown skins, purple-tinged white flesh and a flavor resembling a cross between sweet onion and garlic. A traditional flavoring in the foods of Bordeaux, in southwestern France, they appear in sauces, dressings, marinades and salads. Store them in a cool, dry place, as you would onions or garlic.

TARRAGON

Delicate and sweetly flavored, with a faint hint of licorice, this herb—used both fresh and dried—flavors many French sauces, salads, pickles and egg dishes. Tarragon-flavored white wine vinegar is a popular ingredient in salad dressings.

VERMOUTH

Vermouth takes its name from *Wermut,* the German word for wormwood, an ingredient in many traditional recipes for this commercial, delicately aromatic dry or sweet wine enhanced with herbs and barks. Two of the world's three leading centers for vermouth production are found in France—Marseilles and Chambéry. The wine frequently flavors French sauces and stuffings, and is particularly complementary to seafood and chicken.

TECHNIQUES

The following pages illustrate practical cooking techniques used in this book that may not be familiar to some readers.

SECTIONING ORANGES

When pieces of orange (or other citrus fruits) are called for as a garnish or in a salad or dessert, the oranges must usually be sectioned; that is, their individual sections are freed of the bitter white pith and tough, transparent membranes that surround them. Sectioning is easily accomplished on a cutting board with a sharp knife.

1. CUTTING OFF TOP AND BOTTOM.

Using a small, sharp, thin-bladed knife, cut a slice from the top (stem) end and from the bottom (blossom) end of the orange. Cut them thickly enough to expose the fruit beneath the peel.

2. SLICING OFF THE PEEL.

Steady the fruit upright on the cutting board and, using the knife, slice off the peel all around the fruit. Cut thickly enough to remove the white pith and inner membrane, exposing the fruit sections.

3. CUTTING OUT THE SECTIONS.

Holding the peeled orange over a bowl to catch the fruit and juices, use the knife to free the individual sections, carefully cutting between the fruit and the membranes on either side of each section.

PEELING & SEEDING TOMATOES

Tomatoes are one of the great pleasures of the table—especially at the height of summer, when you should seek out the best sun-ripened tomatoes you can find. At other times of year, plum tomatoes, sometimes called Roma or egg tomatoes, are likely to have the best flavor and texture. Often when tomatoes are made into sauces or combined with other ingredients, recipes call for removing their skins and seeds, neither of which contributes much to the prized flavor or texture of the vegetable-fruit.

1. LOOSENING THE SKIN.

Cut out the core from the stem end of each tomato. Then cut a shallow X in the skin at the tomato's base. Submerge the tomatoes in boiling water for 20–30 seconds. Using a slotted spoon, remove each tomato and submerge in a bowl of cold water.

2. PEELING THE TOMATO.

Starting at the X, peel the skin from each tomato, using your fingertips and, if necessary, the knife blade.

3. SEEDING THE TOMATO.

Cut each tomato in half crosswise. Holding each half over a bowl, squeeze gently to force out the seed sacs. Or use your fingertip or the handle of a small spoon to scoop them out.

TRIMMING & CLEANING LEEKS

Leeks add a wonderfully mild, sweet, oniony flavor to many French dishes. Grown in sandy soil, they frequently have grit trapped between their green leaves and the layers of their white bulb ends. As a result, they require careful cleaning before use in any recipe. The toughest part of the green leaves must be trimmed off as well; and some recipes call for only the white or the white and pale green parts of the vegetable, requiring even further trimming.

1. TRIMMING THE LEEKS.
Using a sharp knife, trim off the root end of each leek. Then, cut off the tough, dark green portions of the leaves, leaving about 1 inch (2.5 cm) of the tender green portion.

2. SLITTING THE LEEKS.
To expose the leek's layers for more thorough cleaning, cut each leek in half lengthwise, starting at the green end and working down the stalk about three-fourths of the way toward the root end.

3. WASHING THE LEEKS.
In a basin filled with cold water, or under a stream of running water, swish the leeks to clean them thoroughly, gently separating the layers with your fingers to wash away any grit or sand trapped inside.

TRUSSING A CHICKEN & TESTING FOR DONENESS

Tying, or trussing, whole poultry before roasting gives it a more compact, uniform shape, ensuring that it cooks more evenly. The result is a bird that not only has moister meat and looks more attractive when presented at table, but is also easier to carve. Many different methods exist for trussing; the one shown here is among the simplest, requiring just a single piece of kitchen string at least long enough to wrap twice lengthwise around the bird. At the earliest possible time the bird might be finished, start checking for doneness with an instant-read thermometer.

1. SECURING DRUMSTICKS.
Place the bird breast-side up and slide the center of the string under its tail. Cross the ends above the tail and loop each around a drumstick; then cross them again (shown here) and pull them tight to draw together the tail and the ends of the drumsticks.

2. COMPLETING TRUSSING.
Turn the bird over and tuck the wing tips across the neck flap. Pull one string along the side, loop it around the nearest wing, pull it tight across the neck flap and loop it around the other wing. Tightly tie together the string ends; cut off any excess string.

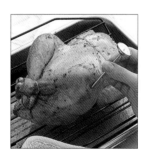

3. TESTING FOR DONENESS.
After roasting, insert an instant-read thermometer into the thickest part of the thigh, taking care not to touch the bone and to insert from above so juices will not run out. A temperature of 180°F (82°C) indicates doneness.

CUTTING CITRUS ZEST

Zest, the thin, brightly colored, outermost layer of a citrus fruit's peel, contains most of the peel's aromatic essential oils—a lively source of flavor for savory and sweet dishes alike. Depending upon how the zest will be combined with other ingredients, how intense a citrus flavor is desired and what decorative effects are called for, the zest may be removed in one of several different ways, shown below. Whichever way you use, take care to remove the colored zest only; the white, spongy pith beneath is bitter and, if included, can mar the flavor of the dish.

GRATING ZEST.
For very fine particles of citrus zest, lightly rub the fruit against the small rasps of a hand-held grater, taking care not to grate away any of the bitter white pith beneath the zest.

SHREDDING ZEST.
Using a simple tool known as a zester, draw its sharp-edged holes across the fruit's skin to remove the zest in thin shreds. Alternatively, use a fine-holed shredder, which has small indented slots to cut shreds.

CUTTING WIDE STRIPS.
Holding the edge of a paring knife or vegetable peeler almost parallel to the fruit's skin, carefully cut off the zest in strips, taking care not to remove any white pith with it.

ROASTING BELL PEPPERS

Bell peppers (capsicums)—especially the ripened red, yellow and orange varieties—have a natural sweetness and a juicy texture that are heightened by roasting. While many different methods exist for roasting peppers, the one shown here streamlines the process by halving, stemming and seeding them first, leaving only the peeling of the blistered skins after the peppers have cooled.

1. HALVING, STEMMING AND SEEDING.
Preheat a broiler (griller) or an oven to 500°F (260°C). Using a small, sharp knife, cut each pepper in half lengthwise. Cut out the stem, seeds and white ribs from each half.

2. ROASTING THE PEPPERS.
Lay the pepper halves, cut side down, on a baking sheet. Place under the broiler or in the oven. Broil (grill) or roast until the skins blister and begin to blacken.

3. PEELING THE PEPPERS.
Remove from the oven and cover with aluminum foil. Let steam until cool enough to handle, 10–15 minutes. Then, using your fingers or a knife, peel off the skins.

ACKNOWLEDGMENTS

I am indebted to the late Thérèse Bacon for introducing me to French cooking in the early 1950s while living in Sonoma; to the chef of the ill-fated luxury liner *Normandie,* whose cooking while resident in San Francisco was inspiring; and to the late James Beard and Elizabeth David, for sharing their varied knowledge of French cooking. I am appreciative of Julia Child for her support and all of the knowledge I have gleaned from her books and television shows, and of René Verdon, Charles Lamalle and the late Henriette Moon, for inspiring me to try new dishes. Lastly, I am particularly grateful to the restaurants in France, and their chefs, where I have eaten so many wonderful meals on my frequent trips during the past 40 years.
I would like to thank John Owen for developing this three-book series; Wendely Harvey for her publishing wisdom; Laurie Wertz, Norman Kolpas and Sharon Silva for their expert editorial work; Allan Rosenberg and Allen Lott for their excellent photography; Heidi Gintner for interpreting the recipes and Sandra Griswold for styling the resulting dishes for the camera; Alice Harth for her wonderful illustrations; John Bull for his creative book design; and everyone else who contributed their time and knowledge to the production of this book.

—Chuck Williams

The publishers would like to thank the following people for their generous assistance and support:
Sharon C. Lott, Stephen W. Griswold, Elaine Anderson, Patty Hill, Tina Schmitz, Ken DellaPenta.

The following kindly lent props for the photography, in San Francisco: Biordi Art Imports, Candelier, Fillamento, Pierre Deux, Sue Fisher King, Linda Larson and Tim Murray of Purcell-Murray Company, Inc., Chuck Williams, Williams-Sonoma (Post Street) and Pottery Barn (Chestnut Street).